Editor
Mara Ellen Guckian

Managing Editor
Ina Massler Levin, M.A.

Editor-in-Chief
Sharon Coan, M.S. Ed.

Illustrator
Sue Fullam

Cover Artist
Denise Bauer

Art Coordinator
Denice Adorno

Imaging
Alfred Lau
Ralph Olmedo, Jr.

Product Manager
Phil Garcia

Publisher
Mary D. Smith, M.S. Ed.

Teaching
Language Arts
through Nursery Rhymes

Includes
Standards &
Benchmarks

Authors

Amy DeCastro, M.A. and Jennifer Kern, M.A.

Teacher
Created
Resources

Teacher Created Resources, Inc.
6421 Industry Way
Westminster, CA 92683
www.teachercreated.com
ISBN 13: 978-0-7439-3010-9
©2001 Teacher Created Resources, Inc.
Reprinted, 2007
Made in U.S.A.

Table of Contents

Introduction

Most children already know many nursery rhymes by heart by the time they reach school. Children love nursery rhymes. They take great delight in the rhyming, rhythm, and familiarity of singing and reciting them. Research shows that reciting nursery rhymes helps children develop phonemic awareness, increases vocabulary and verbal skills, and develops strong auditory discrimination.

Teaching Language Arts through Nursery Rhymes was written to help students develop a conscious understanding of how language works. These lessons can be used with any phonics or reading program to help reinforce learning the alphabet. A template of each letter and rhyme are at the beginning of each lesson. These pages may be copied for students to color or decorate. The alphabet pages could be saved in a folder and turned into an alphabet book. Although the lessons in this book are sequenced alphabetically, there is no specific order in which they need to be taught. Feel free to arrange them to fit your reading or phonics program.

The developmentally appropriate nursery-rhyme activities in this book easily integrate the language arts standards into the curriculum. The activities incorporate the speaking, listening, reading, and writing components of language arts. Such integration enriches learning and makes it meaningful and holistic. With a link to literature, these well-researched, authentic lessons prepare children for the adventure of lifelong learning in an enjoyable way.

This book was organized with easy-to-follow plans that are clear and concise. Lists of suggested materials for each activity are provided at the beginning of each lesson. These materials are generally available in classrooms, teacher supply stores, or grocery stores. There is also a section, Before the Lesson, for each activity to allow for proper setup and to address safety issues. The step-by-step procedures given for students have been tested to ensure their success. Teachers can also feel confident knowing that students are practicing the skills necessary to meet the standards.

The information in this book will provide a wealth of hands-on experiences for young learners. Modify the lessons to fit the needs of your students or your individualized curriculum. Most of all, have fun with language arts!

Nursery Rhyme Scope and Sequence

Language Arts Standards

Nursery Rhyme	Demonstrates competence in general skills and strategies of the writing process	Demonstrates competence in the stylistic and rhetorical aspects of writing	Uses grammatical and mechanical conventions in written compositions	Demonstrates a competence in the general skills and strategies of the reading process	Demonstrates competence in general skills and strategies for reading a variety of literary texts	Demonstrates competence in general skills and strategies for reading a variety of information texts	Demonstrates competence in speaking and listening as tools for learning
This Little Piggie	X	X		X	X	X	X
Yankee Doodle	X			X	X	X	X
Baa, Baa, Black Sheep	X		X	X	X	X	X
Humpty Dumpty	X		X	X	X	X	X
There Was a Crooked Man	X		X	X	X	X	X
Little Boy Blue	X		X	X	X	X	X
Polly Put the Kettle On	X		X	X	X	X	X
Simple Simon	X		X	X	X	X	X
Jack and Jill	X		X	X	X	X	X
Jack Be Nimble	X	X	X	X	X	X	X
Little Bo-Peep	X	X	X	X	X	X	X
Old Woman in a Shoe	X		X	X	X	X	X
Little Nut Tree	X	X	X	X	X		X
Little Miss Muffet	X		X	X	X		X
Mary Had a Little Lamb	X		X	X	X		X
Georgie Porgie	X		X	X	X		X
Diddle, Diddle, Dumpling	X	X	X	X	X		X
Little Jack Horner	X		X	X	X		X
Pease Porridge Hot	X	X	X	X	X	X	X
Mary, Mary, Quite Contrary	X		X	X	X	X	X
Three Little Kittens	X		X	X	X	X	X
Peter, Peter, Pumpkin Eater	X		X	X	X	X	X
Hey Diddle, Diddle	X	X	X	X	X	X	X
Hickory, Dickory, Dock	X	X	X	X	X	X	X
Three Men in a Tub	X	X	X	X	X	X	X
Ring-Around-the-Rosies	X	X	X	X	X	X	X

Learning the Alphabet with Nursery Rhymes

A, around, all around! Ring-around-the-rosies and we all fall down.

B, the butcher and the baker, in a tub with the candlestick maker.

C, clock, hickory, dickory, dock. The mouse ran up as it went tick, tock.

D, diddle, hey diddle, diddle. What's a cow to do with a cat and a fiddle?

E, eat, what a treat! Peter's pumpkin is very sweet!

F, find, find your mittens. Find your mittens, you naughty kittens.

G, grow, how does your garden grow? If you don't water it, you'll never know.

H, hot, pease porridge hot. What if it's cold? I hope it's not.

I, I, what a good boy am I, said Little Jack Horner with his thumb in a pie.

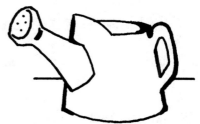

J, John, Little Dumpling John, had one shoe off and one shoe on.

K, kiss, Georgie Porgie, pudding and pie, kissed the girls and made them cry.

L, lamb, Mary's little lamb followed her to school. Now she's in a jam.

M, Muffet, Little Miss, would not give that spider a kiss.

Learning the Alphabet with Nursery Rhymes <small>(cont.)</small>

N, nutmeg, nutmeg and pear, would my little nut tree bear.

O, old, old woman in a shoe, had so many kids, what's she going to do?

P, peep, Little Bo-Peep. If she's not careful, she'll lose her sheep.

Q, quick, Jack be quick. Jack jump over the candlestick.

R, run, run up the hill. But don't fall down with Jack and Jill.

S, Simon, Simple Simon, we all know he met a pieman.

T, tea, let's all have tea. Polly put the kettle on for you and me.

U, under, under the hay. Little Boy Blue was sleeping away.

V, very crooked mouse and a crooked man in a crooked house.

W, wall, off the wall. Humpty Dumpty had a great fall.

X, extra, have you any wool? Yes sir, yes sir, three bags full.

Y, Yankee, Doodle dee dee, went to town on his little pony.

Z, zero roast beef had he, for the little piggie who went wee, wee, wee.

Ring-Around-the-Rosies

Ring-around-the-rosies

A pocket full of posies

Ashes, ashes,

We all fall down!

Ring-Around-the-Rosies (cont.)

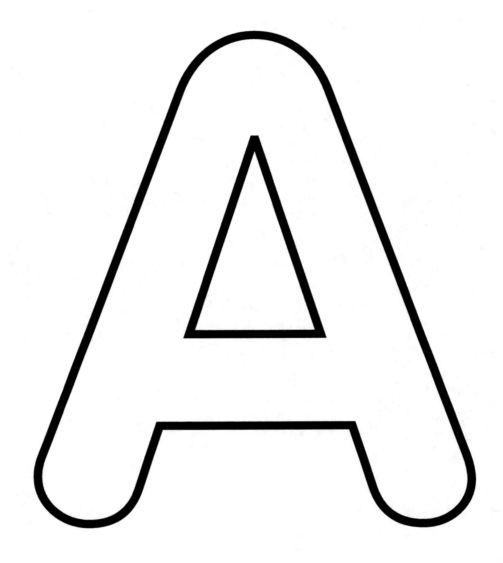

"A," around, all around! Ring-around-
the-rosies and we all fall down.

Ring-Around-the-Rosies (cont.)

Lesson

Skills

- long vowel recognition
- short vowel recognition

Materials

- vowel pockets (page 10)
- craft sticks
- scissors
- glue
- posie pictures (pages 11–14)
- poster board

Before the Lesson

1. Copy the nursery rhyme "Ring-Around-the-Rosies" from page 7 onto chart paper or enlarge it so that the class can see the words easily.

2. Prepare five vowel pockets using the pattern found on page 10. Write a different vowel letter on each pocket. Cut them out and glue them to the poster board, leaving an opening at the top.

3. Cut out the posie pictures found on pages 11–14 and glue each one to a craft stick. Separate the long and short vowel-sound pictures.

Procedure

1. Read the nursery rhyme "Ring-Around-the-Rosies" to the class, using the larger display version. Read the rhyme again, tracking the words and allowing the class to join in if they are familiar with the rhyme.

2. Introduce the five vowels to the class. Share that these are special letters that make more than one sound. Vowels are special letters because they make two sounds. They can make short sounds such as in a-pple, e-gg, i-gloo, o-strich, and u-mbrella. When vowels say their names, they are called long vowels (a-pe, e-leven, i-ce cream, o-pen, u-nicorn). Go over each letter and the vowel sounds one by one.

3. Display the pockets poster and tell the students that the pockets need to be filled with posies. One at a time, allow each student to come up and pick up a posie and place it in the correct vowel pocket.

Ring-Around-the-Rosies <small>(cont.)</small>

Vowel Pocket

Directions: Make five pockets and write a different vowel on each one.

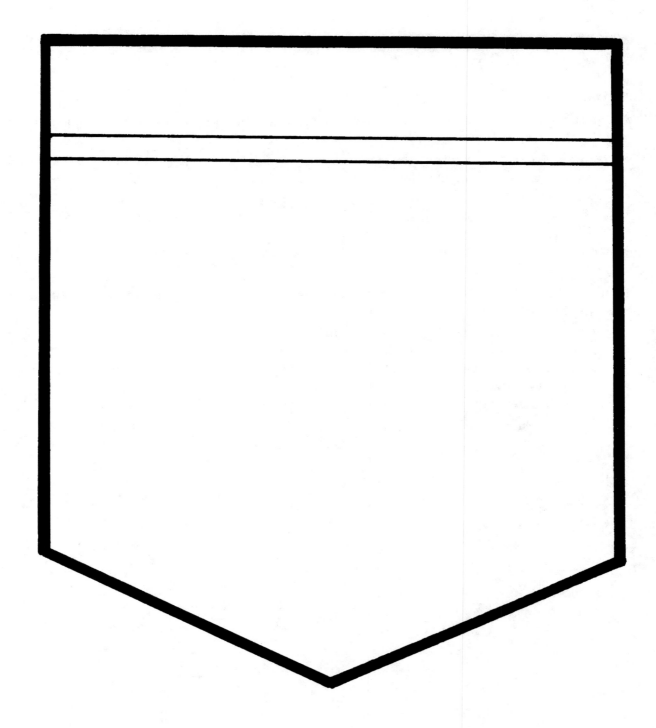

Ring-Around-the-Rosies (cont.)

Directions: Cut out the posies and use them with the vowel
pockets on page 10.

overalls

octopus

Indian

ice cream

umbrella

insect

Ring-Around-the-Rosies (cont.)

Directions: Cut out the posies and use them with the vowel pockets on page 10.

12

Ring-Around-the-Rosies (cont.)

Directions: Cut out the posies and use them with the vowel pockets on page 10.

Ring-Around-the-Rosies *(cont.)*

Directions: Cut out the posies and use them with the vowel pockets on page 10.

Three Men in a Tub

Rub a dub-dub

Three men in a tub,

And who do you think they be?

The butcher, the baker,

The candlestick maker.

Turn 'em out, knaves all three.

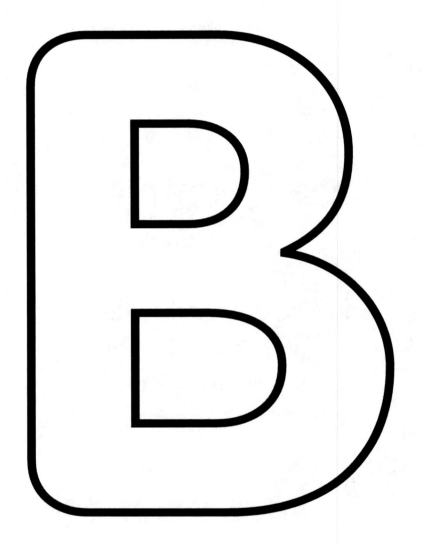

"B," the butcher and the baker,
in a tub with the candlestick maker.

Three Men in a Tub (cont.)

Lesson

Skills
- character and setting identification
- role playing

Materials
- crayons
- tub cutout (page 19), one per student
- scissors
- three men cutouts (page 18), one per student

Before the Lesson
1. Copy the nursery rhyme "Three Men in a Tub" from page 15 onto chart paper or enlarge it so that the class can see the words easily.

2. Make one copy of the setting (tub) on page 19 and one copy of the characters (three men) found on page 18 for each student.

Procedure
1. Read the nursery rhyme "Three Men in a Tub," using the enlarged version of the rhyme. Read the rhyme a second time, tracking the words and allowing the students to join in if they already know the words.

2. Explain to the students that the *characters* are usually the people and/or animals in a story, song, or poem. Ask the students to identify the characters in the rhyme "Three Men in a Tub." (*butcher, baker,* and *candlestick maker*) Take this opportunity to discuss the three men's occupations and, perhaps, to discuss other occupations as well.

3. Next, explain that the setting in a story, song, or poem is the place where the action occurs. Ask the students to identify the setting in the poem. (*tub*)

4. Distribute the story element cutouts found on pages 18 and 19. Allow the students to color and cut out each of the characters and the tub. (Students may need help cutting the slot in the tub.)

5. Allow the students to role-play the rhyme with their cutouts while identifying the characters and the setting.

Three Men in a Tub (cont.)

Characters

Directions: Cut out and color the three characters below.

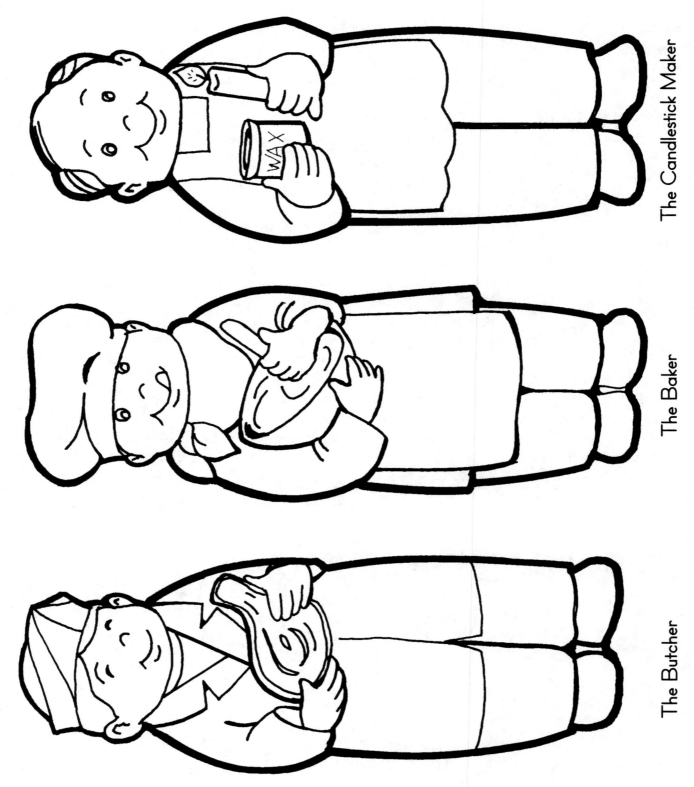

The Candlestick Maker

The Baker

The Butcher

Three Men in a Tub (cont.)

Setting

Directions: Cut out the tub and color it. Cut along the dotted line to make a slit for the three men.

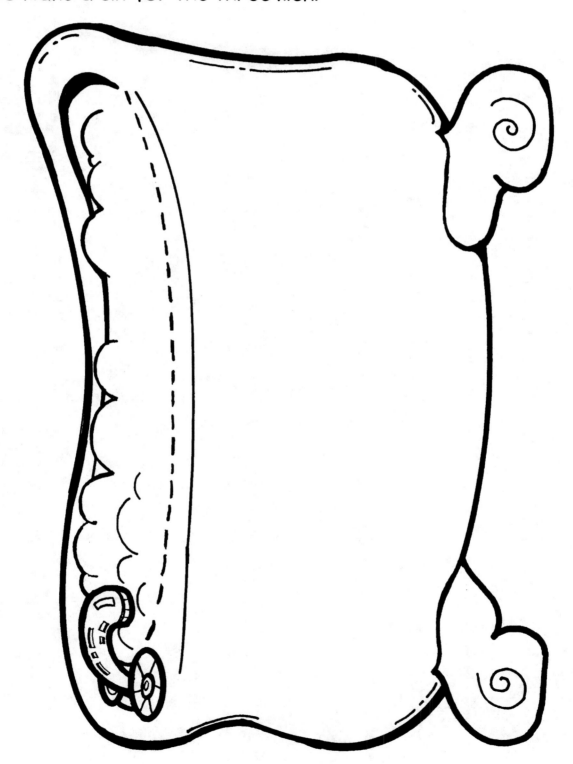

Hickory, Dickory, Dock

Hickory, dickory, dock,

The mouse ran up the clock.

The clock struck one,

The mouse ran down,

Hickory, dickory, dock.

Hickory, Dickory, Dock (cont.)

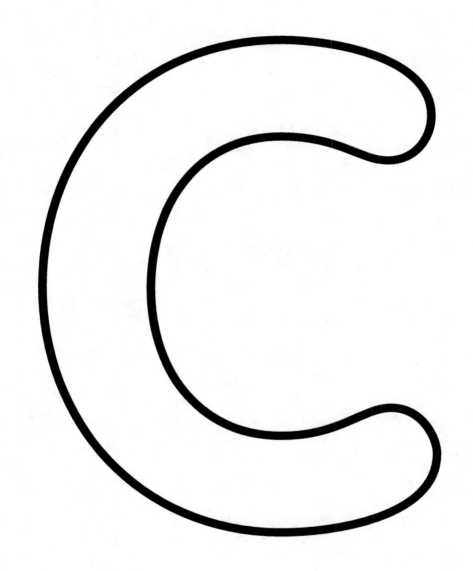

"C," clock, hickory, dickory, dock. The mouse ran up as it went tick, tock.

Hickory, Dickory, Dock *(cont.)*

Lesson 1

Skill

- letter recognition

Materials

- 1 small cube or block for every 3–4 students
- game board (page 23), one per student
- puzzle pieces sheet (page 24), one per student
- scissors

Before the Lesson

1. Copy a game board and a puzzle pieces page for each student.
2. Write the capital letters M-O-U-S-E on each small cube or block to create dice or "mouse rollers."

Procedure

1. Read the nursery rhyme "Hickory, Dickory, Dock," using the enlarged version of the rhyme. Read the rhyme a second time, tracking the words and allowing the students to join in if they already know the words.

2. Share with the students that the mouse is the character in the rhyme. Write the word "MOUSE" in all capital letters on chart paper or a chalkboard, saying each letter as you write it.

3. Underneath the capital letters, write the word "mouse" in lowercase letters, again repeating each letter as it is written.

4. Have students divide up into groups of three or four and explain how to play the game "Mouse Match." Each student receives a game board and one puzzle pieces sheet. Each group shares a prepared "mouse roller."

   A. Cut the puzzle piece sheet along the dotted lines and stack the pieces in a pile.

   B. Take turns rolling the "mouse roller." Match the uppercase letter rolled with the "mouse roller" to the matching lowercase letter puzzle pieces.

   C. Place the puzzle piece on the appropriate section of the game board.

   D. Continue rolling the "mouse roller" and matching puzzle pieces to complete the page. When all the capital and lowercase letters have been matched, a picture will be revealed.

Note: Players lose a turn if they roll letters previously used. If a player lands on the blank side of the "mouse roller," or on a letter they have already rolled, he or she loses a turn.

Hickory, Dickory, Dock (cont.)

	E
	S
	U
	O
	M

Hickory, Dickory, Dock (cont.)

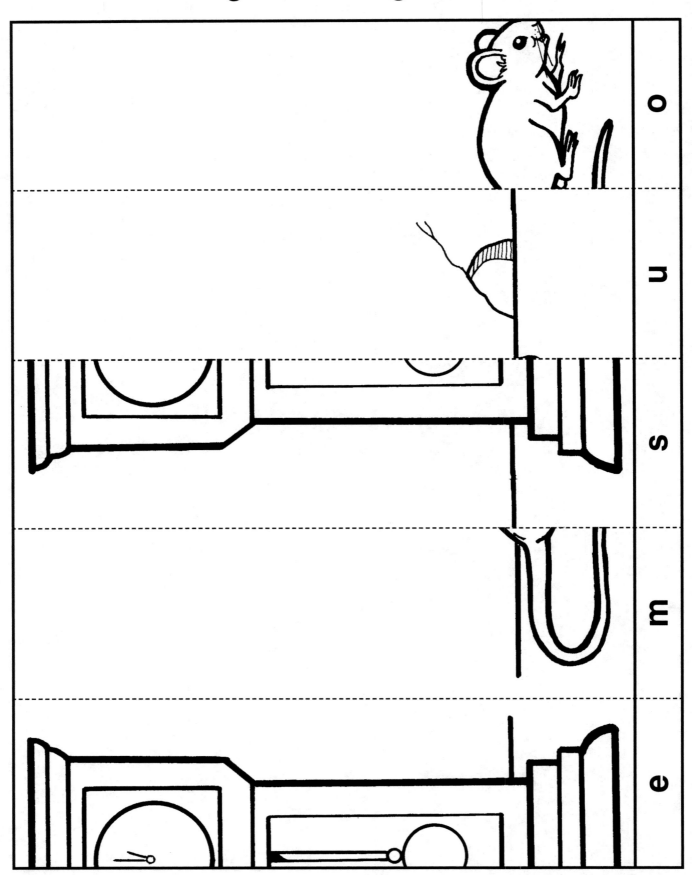

Hickory, Dickory, Dock (cont.)

Lesson 2

Skill

- short vowel recognition

Materials

- Short Vowels activity (page 26), one per student
- alphabet stamps or alphabet stickers or magazines
- markers

Before the Lesson

1. Make one copy of the Short Vowel activity page for each student.

Procedure

1. Read the nursery rhyme "Hickory, Dickory, Dock," using the enlarged version of the rhyme. Read the rhyme a second time, tracking the words and allowing the students to join in.

2. Review the two kinds of letters in the alphabet, *vowels* and *consonants*. Explain that the five vowels—A, E, I, O, and U—have more than one sound. When vowels say their names they are called *long vowels* (a-pe, e-leven, ice cream, o-pen, u-nicorn). When the vowels do not say their names they are called *short vowels*.

3. Give each vowel an action to help students remember the short sounds.

"A" for a-a-alligator	*Hold arms out in front, moving them like an alligator's mouth opening and closing. Open each time the short sound is emphasized.*
"E" for e-e-elephant	*Hold one arm up in front of your nose moving it like the trunk of an elephant.*
"I" for i-i-itching	*Scratch head with fingertips.*
"O" for o-o-octopus	*Wave arms to the side and then to the front like tentacles.*
"U" for u-u-umbrella	*Pretend to hold an umbrella in hands.*

4. Give the students different examples of words and ask them to identify the short vowel sound they hear at the beginning of each word. (Examples: egg, off, it, ask, under)

5. Next, give the students different examples of words and ask them to identify the short vowel sound they hear in the middle of the word. (Examples: sit, mat, cup, bed, box)

6. Read the nursery rhyme a final time. As you say the rhyme, have the students identify the short vowel sounds they hear in the words *hickory, dickory, dock, the mouse ran up the clock*.

7. Finally, give each student the short vowel activity found on page 26. With different forms of media for them to choose (alphabet stamps or markers, alphabet stickers, or cutout letters from magazines or newspapers), have the students identify and fill in the missing short vowels.

Hickory, Dickory, Dock (cont.)

Lesson 2 *(cont.)*

Short Vowels

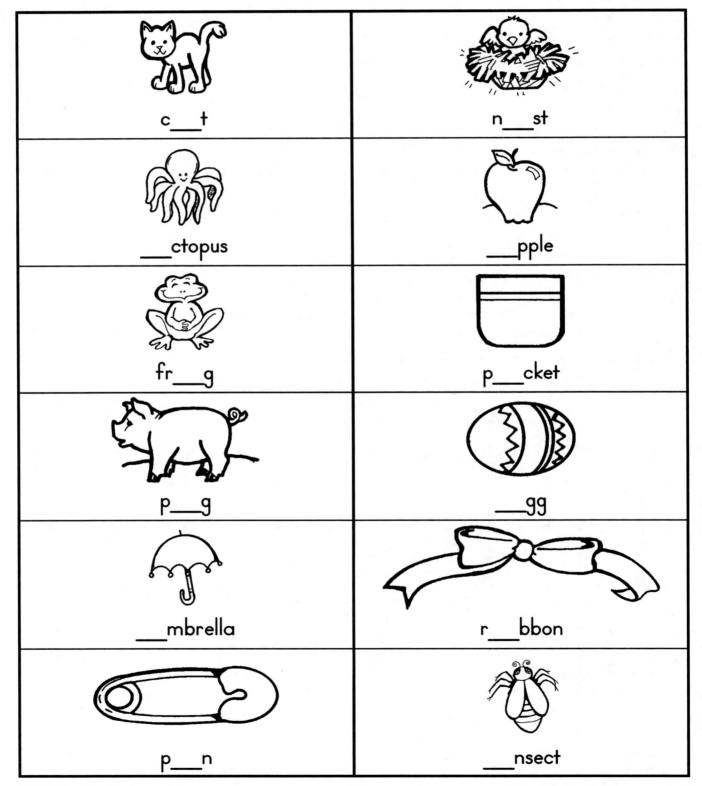

c__t

n___st

___ctopus

___pple

fr___g

p___cket

p__g

___gg

___mbrella

r___bbon

p___n

___nsect

Hey Diddle, Diddle

Hey diddle, diddle,

The cat and the fiddle,

The cow jumped over the moon.

The little dog laughed

To see such a sport,

And the dish

Ran away with the spoon.

Hey Diddle, Diddle (cont.)

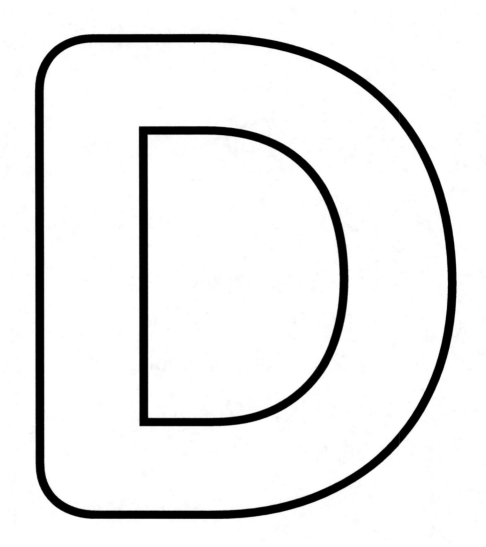

"D," diddle, hey diddle, diddle.
What's a cow to do with a cat
and a fiddle?

Hey Diddle, Diddle *(cont.)*

Lesson 1

Skill
- role playing

Materials
- cow, cat, fiddle, dog, dish, and spoon puppet patterns (pages 30–32), one set per group of students
- tongue depressors, one per student
- crayons
- scissors
- glue
- paper plate
- aluminum foil

Before the Lesson
1. Copy the set of puppet patterns for each group.
2. Color, cut, and laminate one set of puppets for the classroom.
3. Copy and enlarge the nursery rhyme "Hey Diddle, Diddle."
4. Cover the paper plate with aluminum foil. Use the foil-covered plate for the moon.

Procedure
1. Read the nursery rhyme "Hey Diddle, Diddle," using the enlarged version of the rhyme. Read the rhyme a second time, tracking the words and allowing the students to join in.
2. Share the classroom set of puppets with the students. See if the class can say the rhyme as the appropriate puppets are held up.
3. Divide the class into groups of seven. Give each student in the group a different puppet character.
4. Allow the students to color, cut out, and glue their characters to tongue depressors to create puppets.
5. As the students finish, say the rhyme one more time. Demonstrate for the class, using one group, how to act out the rhyme with the puppets.
6. Allow the students to role-play on their own while saying the rhyme. Encourage the students to mimic the actions of the characters while saying the words.
7. After they have acted out the rhyme a few times, invite the students to trade puppets.

Hey Diddle, Diddle *(cont.)*

Directions: Color and cut out the dish and the spoon. Attach the dish and the spoon to tongue depressors.

Hey Diddle, Diddle (cont.)

Directions: Color and cut out the cat and the fiddle. Attach the cat and the fiddle to tongue depressors.

Hey Diddle, Diddle (cont.)

Directions: Color and cut out the cow and the dog. Attach the cow and the dog to tongue depressors.

Hey Diddle, Diddle (cont.)

Lesson 2

Skill
- letter/sound connection

Materials
- Hey Diddle, Diddle Letter Book (pages 34–35), one set per student
- magazines and newspapers
- crayons
- scissors
- glue

Before the Lesson
1. Have a volunteer copy, cut, and staple together one mini-book for each student.
2. Set out scissors, magazines, and newspapers.
3. Enlarge the rhyme "Hey Diddle, Diddle."

Procedure
1. Read the nursery rhyme "Hey Diddle, Diddle," using the enlarged version of the rhyme. Read the rhyme a second time, tracking the words and allowing the students to join in when they feel comfortable.
2. Discuss the characters in the rhyme (*cat, fiddle, cow, moon, dog, dish,* and *spoon*). Point to the character words and have the students notice the beginning letters. Do the same with the ending letters.
3. Point to other items in the classroom and have the students identify the beginning and ending letters.
4. Give each student a copy of the "Hey Diddle, Diddle Letter Book." Point out that some of the letters are missing under each picture.
5. Have the students determine which letters are missing on each page of their book. Then, have them locate in the magazines the missing beginning and ending letters and cut out the letters.
6. The cutout letters can then be glued into the appropriate boxes under the pictures.
7. When all the letters have been filled in, allow students to color their books.

Hey Diddle, Diddle
Letter Book

by _____

o

o o

a

Hey Diddle, Diddle (cont.)

		o	

	i	s	h

s	p	o	o

i	d	d	e

Peter, Peter, Pumpkin Eater

Peter, Peter, pumpkin eater,

Had a wife and couldn't

Keep her.

He put her in a pumpkin shell,

And there he kept her very well.

Peter, Peter, Pumpkin Eater (cont.)

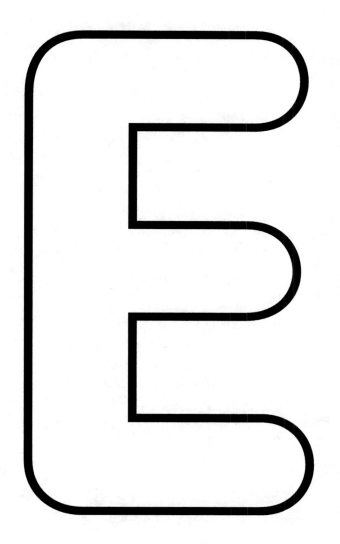

"E," eat, what a treat!
Peter's pumpkin is very sweet!

Peter, Peter, Pumpkin Eater *(cont.)*

Lesson 1

Skill
- sequencing

Materials
- sequencing page (page 39), one per student
- crayons
- scissors
- 8½" x 11" (22 cm x 28 cm) copy paper
- glue sticks

Before the Lesson
1. Copy the sequencing page found on page 39 for each student.

Procedure
1. Read the nursery rhyme "Peter, Peter, Pumpkin Eater," using the enlarged version of the rhyme. Read the rhyme a second time, tracing the words and allowing the students to join in.

2. Discuss what sequencing means. Explain that when you sequence items, you put them in order. Familiarize the students with the vocabulary *first*, *next*, and *last*.
   - Have three students stand in line at the door. Ask the class who is first, next, and who is last?
   - Mention the meals of the day: breakfast, lunch, and dinner. Ask the students which one is eaten first? next? last?
   - Compare a baby, a teenager, and a grandparent. Ask the students what they were first, what they will be next, and what they will be last?

3. Tell the students that they will be sequencing the rhyme "Peter, Peter, Pumpkin Eater" by showing what happened first, next, and then last.

4. Pass out the materials and allow the students to cut out the three rhyme pictures on the page.

5. Ask them to paste the pictures of the rhyme onto the strip in the order it occurred.

6. After you have checked each student's story strip for comprehension, allow each to color and decorate his or her work.

Breakfast

Lunch

Dinner

Peter, Peter, Pumpkin Eater (cont.)

Had a wife and couldn't keep her.

3.

Put her in a pumpkin shell, and there he kept her very well!

2.

Peter, Peter, pumpkin eater

1.

Peter, Peter, Pumpkin Eater (cont.)

Lesson 2

Skill

- identify words that use alliteration

Materials

- copy of "Peter, Peter, Pumpkin Eater" nursery rhyme (page 36)
- chart paper or butcher paper
- copy of the writing activity page (page 42), one per student
- one cover page for a class book (page 41)

Before the Lesson

Copy or enlarge the nursery rhyme "Peter, Peter, Pumpkin Eater" onto chart paper or butcher paper so that the entire class will be able to view the rhyme as it is read.

Procedure

1. Read the nursery rhyme "Peter, Peter, Pumpkin Eater" to the class. Read the rhyme again, tracking the words that have been recreated on chart paper. Invite the students who know the rhyme to join in reading it with you.

2. Ask the students what it was that Peter ate. (*pumpkin*) Share that Peter and pumpkin both begin with the letter "p." Encourage the students to come up with other "p" words that Peter could have eaten instead of a pumpkin. (*popcorn, pizza, pickles, prunes, plums, pie, peaches, pretzels,* etc.) Explain to students that alliteration refers to similar sounds. In this case, the similar sounds are the beginnings of the words they are naming.

3. Repeat the first line, substituting the new word in place of pumpkin. (Peter, Peter, Popcorn Eater. Peter, Peter, Pizza Eater.)

4. Ask each student to come up with a food item that begins with the same beginning letter as his or her first name. Use examples of names of children not in the room to get them started. (*Freddie, Freddie, French Fry Eater. Toby, Toby, Taco Eater,* etc.)

5. After each child has his or her alliteration ready, have them share their responses orally.

6. Finally, have the students write and illustrate their responses on writing activity page found on page 42. Combine all the pages to create a class alliteration book.

Our Class Version
of
Peter, Peter, Pumpkin Eater

by _____

Peter, Peter, Pumpkin Eater <small>(cont.)</small>

_____, _____,
          Name   Name

_____ Eater
             Food

Three Little Kittens

Three little kittens
They lost their mittens,
And they began to cry.
Oh, mother dear, we sadly fear
Our mittens we have lost.
What, lost your mittens?
You naughty kittens!
Then you shall have no pie.
Mee-ow, mee-ow, mee-ow,
Then you shall have no pie.

The three little kittens,
They found their mittens,
And they began to cry.
Oh mother dear, see here, see here,
Our mittens we have found.
Put on your mittens,
You silly kittens,
And you shall have some pie.
Purr-r, purr-r, purr-r
Oh, let us have some pie.

Three Little Kittens (cont.)

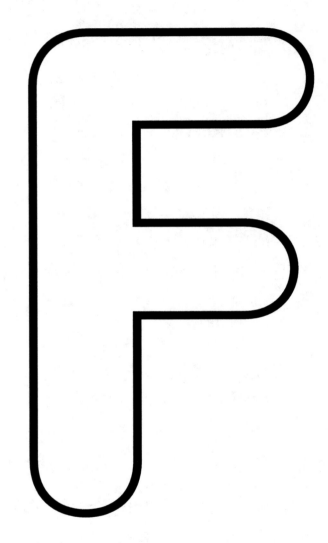

"F," find, find your mittens.

Find your mittens, you naughty kittens.

Three Little Kittens (cont.)

Lesson

Skill

- creative writing

Materials

- butcher paper or chart paper
- pencils and paper
- pictures of pets

Before the Lesson

1. Enlarge the "Three Little Kittens" nursery rhyme onto butcher paper or chart paper and display it in the classroom so that students can view it easily.

2. Gather pictures of different house pets, including kittens.

Procedure

1. Read the nursery rhyme "Three Little Kittens," using the enlarged version of the rhyme. Read the rhyme a second time, tracking the words and allowing the students to join in.

2. Choose from the following to discuss and use as writing (dictation) prompts for the students.

    - Talk about kittens being pets. Have the students brainstorm other animals that could be pets. List their suggestions on chart paper. Show the students the pet pictures and match them to the words on the chart. Then, ask each student to write or dictate a story about his or her pet. If a student does not have a pet, suggest he or she write about a pet he or she would like to own.

    - Ask the students what it was that the kittens in the nursery rhyme lost. Ask each student to share a time when he or she lost something. Ask if the item lost was ever found and if so, how he or she felt. Finally, have the students write about their experiences.

    - Ask the students why it was that the kittens were crying. Ask what emotion the kittens were feeling? (*sad*) Brainstorm other emotions that people have. (*happy, excited, scared, embarrassed, grouchy, nervous, angry, proud*) Have students take turns showing facial expressions to mimic the different emotions mentioned. Then, have each student pick one emotion and write (or dictate) a story about a time he or she experienced that emotion. Encourage the students to share what caused those feelings.

Mary, Mary, Quite Contrary

Mary, Mary,

Quite contrary,

How does your garden grow?

With silver bells

And cockle shells,

And pretty maids all in a row.

Mary, Mary, Quite Contrary (cont.)

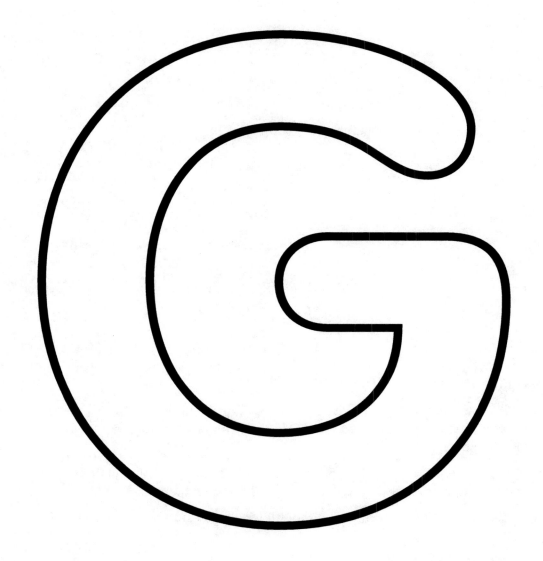

"G," grow, how does your garden grow?

If you don't water it, you'll never know.

Mary, Mary, Quite Contrary (cont.)

Lesson

Skill

- color words recognition

Materials

- crayons—red, brown, orange, yellow, pink, blue, purple, and green
- Flowers cutouts (page 49), one per student
- Flowerpots cutouts (page 50), one per student
- scissors
- glue

Before the Lesson

1. Copy the nursery rhyme "Mary, Mary, Quite Contrary" onto chart paper or enlarge it so that the class can see the words easily.

2. Make one copy of the Flowers and Flowerpots pages for each student. Gather appropriate crayons.

Procedure

1. Read the nursery rhyme "Mary, Mary, Quite Contrary," using the enlarged version of the rhyme. Read the rhyme a second time, tracking the words and allowing the students to join in if they already know the words.

2. Pass out the Flowerpots pages. Have the students color all the pots brown. Review the color words with the students as they read the labels on each pot. Mention that they will be coloring a flower to match each pot.

3. Instruct the students to color each flower on the Flowers page a different color (red, blue, pink, yellow, green, purple, orange). The colors offered should match the flowerpot labels.

4. Have the students cut out the flowers and the flowerpots. (Students may need help cutting the slit in the pots.)

5. Have the students read the color word on the pot and find the matching flower color. When each flower has been placed in the appropriate pot, glue the pair to a large piece of paper. If time allows, students can decorate around the pots. Grass could be drawn, or a shelf for the pots to rest on, or a windowsill.

Mary, Mary, Quite Contrary (cont.)

Flowers

Directions: Color each flower a different color, using red, blue, pink, yellow, purple, and orange. Color the leaves and stems green. Cut out the flowers.

Mary, Mary, Quite Contrary (cont.)

Flowerpots

Directions: Color each pot and cut it out. Glue the matching (same color) flower (page 49) to each pot.

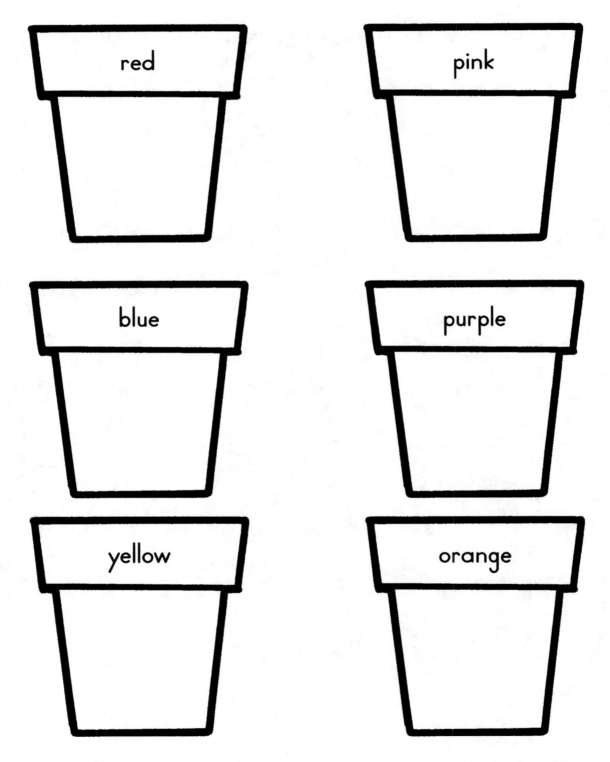

Pease Porridge Hot

Pease porridge hot,

Pease porridge cold,

Pease porridge in the pot,

Nine days old.

Some like it hot,

Some like it cold,

Some like it in the pot,

Nine days old.

Pease Porridge Hot (cont.)

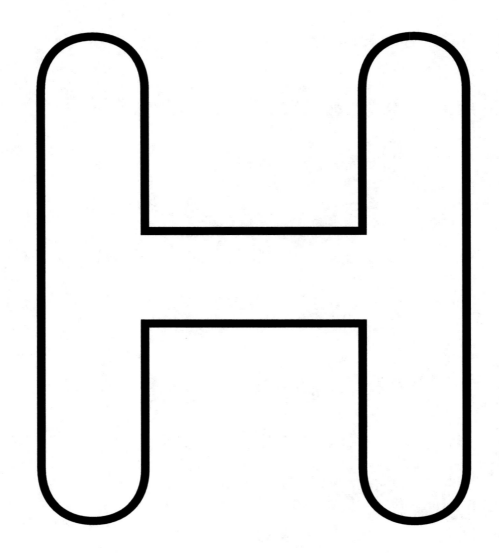

"H," hot, pease porridge hot.
What if it's cold? I hope it's not!

Pease Porridge Hot (cont.)

Lesson

Skill
- recognition of opposites

Materials
- sets of Opposites Cards (pages 54–55), one set per 3–4 students
- chart paper for brainstorming opposites

Before the Lesson
1. Copy the nursery rhyme "Pease Porridge Hot" onto chart paper or enlarge it so that the class can see the words easily.
2. Copy and laminate sets of Opposites Cards for each group of students.
3. Label the chart paper "Opposites."

Procedure
1. Read the nursery rhyme "Pease Porridge Hot" to the class, using the larger display version. Read the rhyme again, tracking the words and allowing the students to join in if they are familiar with the rhyme.
2. Ask the students to identify the two words in the rhyme that are opposites. (*hot and cold*) Give other examples of opposites.
3. Ask the students to come up with other words that are opposites. Write their answers on the chart paper.
4. Divide the students up into groups of 3–4 to play the "Opposites Memory Game." Pass out one set of Opposite Cards to each group. Have the students turn each card facedown and then rearrange them. The students will take turns flipping over two cards. If the two cards are opposites, they get to keep them.

Pease Porridge Hot (cont.)

Opposites Cards (cont.)

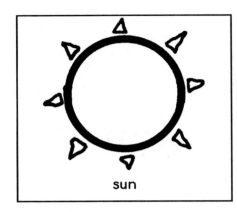

sun

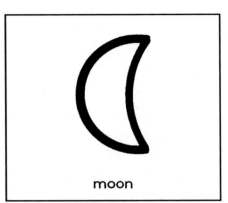

moon

boy

girl

hairy

bald

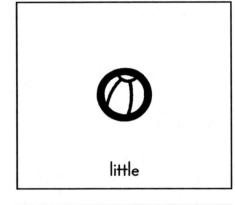

little

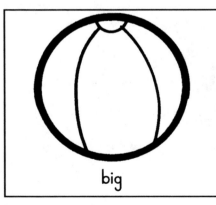

big

inside

outside

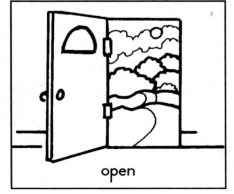

open

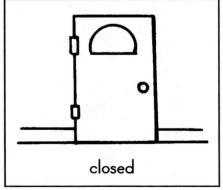

closed

Pease Porridge Hot (cont.)

Opposites Cards (cont.)

happy

sad

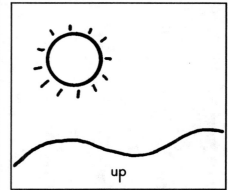

up

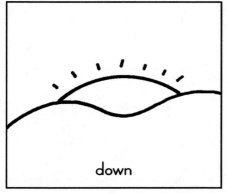

down

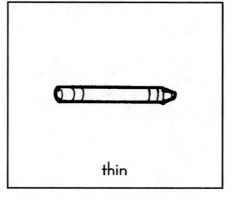

thin

thick

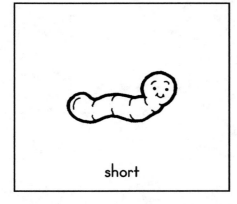

short

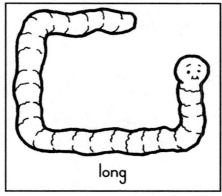

long

sweet

sour

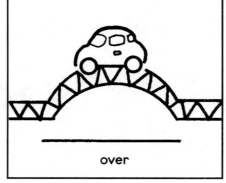

over

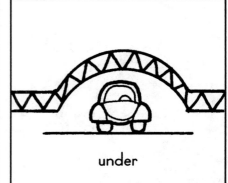

under

Little Jack Horner

Little Jack Horner

Sat in a corner,

Eating a Christmas pie.

He put in his thumb,

And pulled out a plum,

And said,

What a good boy am I!

Little Jack Horner (cont.)

"I," I, what a good boy am I, said Little Jack Horner with his thumb in a pie.

Little Jack Horner (cont.)

Lesson 1

Skills
- sequencing

Materials
- Sequencing Cards, page 59, one per student
- Flip-Book Pattern, page 60, one per student
- 8½" x 11" (22 cm x 28 cm) copy paper
- crayons
- glue sticks
- scissors

Before the Lesson
1. Make one copy of the flip-book pattern for each student.
2. Copy the sequencing cards worksheet for each student.
3. Prepare a flip book. If possible, laminate for later use in a center or reading area.

Procedure
1. Read the nursery rhyme "Little Jack Horner," using the enlarged version of the rhyme. Read the rhyme a second time, tracking the words and allowing the students to join in.
2. Review the definition of sequencing (e.g., to put things in order).
3. Tell the students that they will be sequencing the rhyme of "Little Jack Horner."
4. Show the students the premade flip book and sequencing cards.
5. Have the students color the three pictures and cut them out. Read the captions with the students and discuss the pictures.
6. Discuss the sequence of events. Focus on the words *first, next,* and *last.* Have the students arrange the pictures in sequential order and glue them into the appropriate boxes on the strip.
7. Give each student a flip-book pattern and guide him or her in folding the page so that the numbers are on top. Have students cut on the two dotted lines.
8. Glue the completed story strip to the inside of the flip book.
9. Demonstrate how to lift the numbered flaps to "read" the rhyme. Encourage students to share their books with their families.

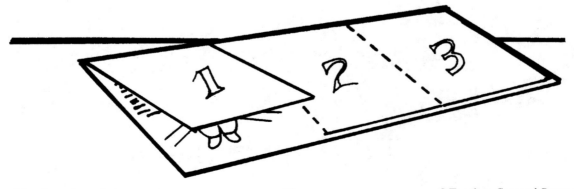

Little Jack Horner (cont.)

Sequencing Cards

Directions: Cut out the three cards and put them in the order they occur in the rhyme. Glue them onto the numbered strip. Place the completed strip inside the folded flip book.

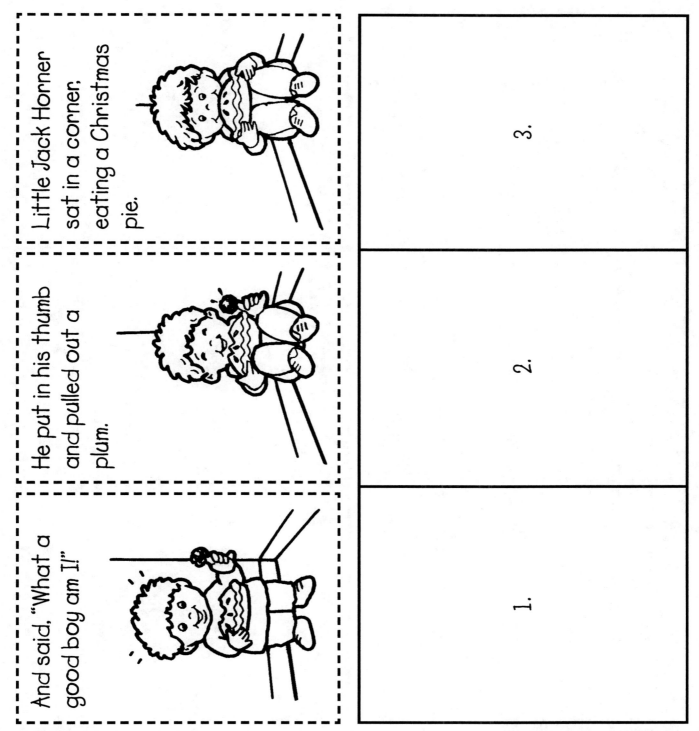

Little Jack Horner sat in a corner, eating a Christmas pie.

He put in his thumb and pulled out a plum.

And said, "What a good boy am I!"

3.

2.

1.

Little Jack Horner (cont.)

Flip-book Pattern

Directions: Fold the paper along the solid line (hot dog style). The numbers should be on top. Carefully cut the two dotted lines. Place the completed story strip (page 59) inside.

Little Jack Horner (cont.)

Lesson 2

Skill
- letter recognition

Materials
- 1 pie tin
- copies of "plum letters" (pages 62–65)
- sticky tack or clay molded into the shape of a thimble, or double-stick tape
- purple construction paper

Before the Lesson
1. Copy the nursery rhyme "Little Jack Horner" onto chart paper or enlarge it so the class can see the words easily.

2. Copy the plum letters onto purple construction paper. Laminate and cut out the plums and put them into the pie tin.

Procedure
1. Read the nursery rhyme "Little Jack Horner" to the class, using the larger display version. Read the rhyme again, tracking the words and allowing the students to join in if they are familiar with the rhyme.

2. Next, explain to the students that they will be playing a letter game. In the game, they will do what Jack Horner did in the rhyme.

3. Have the students sit in a circle. Explain that they will go around the circle and that each student will have a chance to "put in his or her thumb and pull out a plum." To do this they will take turns wearing the sticky-tack thimble.
   Variation: Place a piece of double-stick tape on each child's finger instead of having the students take turns with the thimble.

4. Introduce the pie tin filled with letters to the students and have them begin passing it around the circle. The first time the pie pan goes around the circle, say the rhyme together. Then choose someone to start pulling out the plums.

5. Each student will put the sticky-tack thimble on his or her thumb to pick up a capital letter. Once that student has a letter they must tell what the letter is and the sound the letter makes. They may ask a friend if they need some help.

6. Once the student says the letter and makes the correct letter sound, the class will say, "What a good boy/girl you are!" He or she may hold that letter until the end of the game.

7. Go around the circle until all of the capital letters have been picked up.

8. If time permits repeat the lesson using the lowercase letters or have the students find the matching uppercase letter for the lowercase letter pulled from the pie.

Little Jack Horner (cont.)

Uppercase Letters

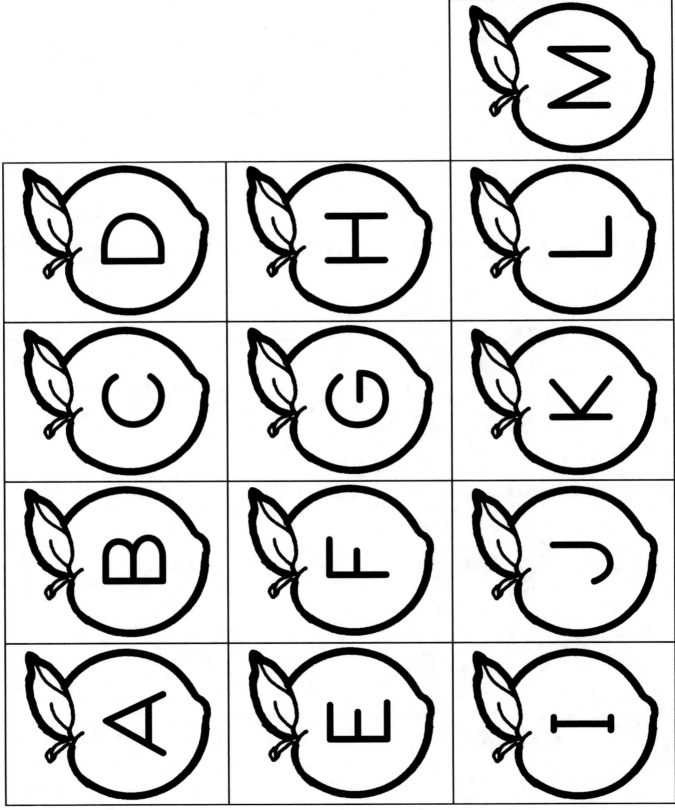

Little Jack Horner (cont.)

Uppercase Letters (cont.)

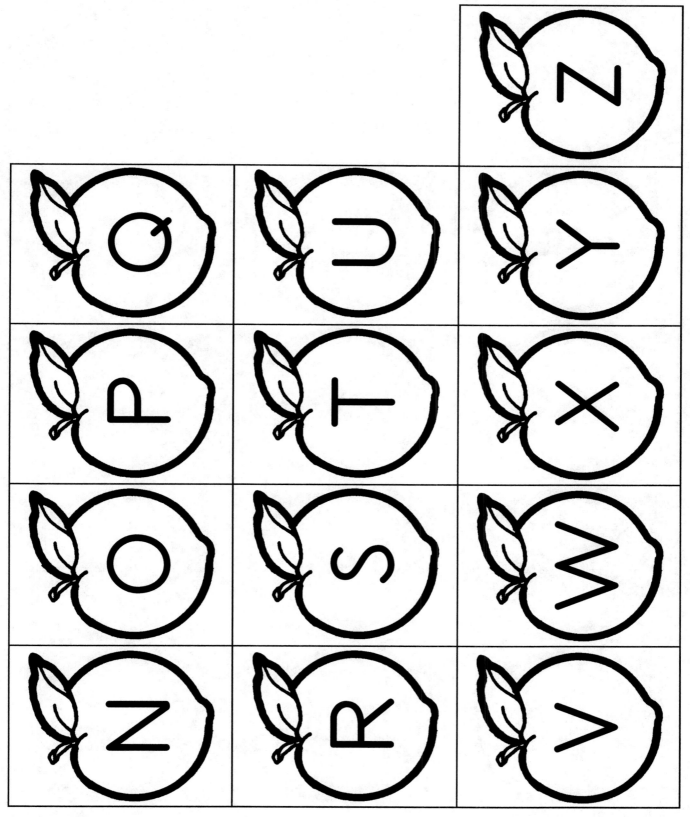

Little Jack Horner (cont.)

Lowercase Letters

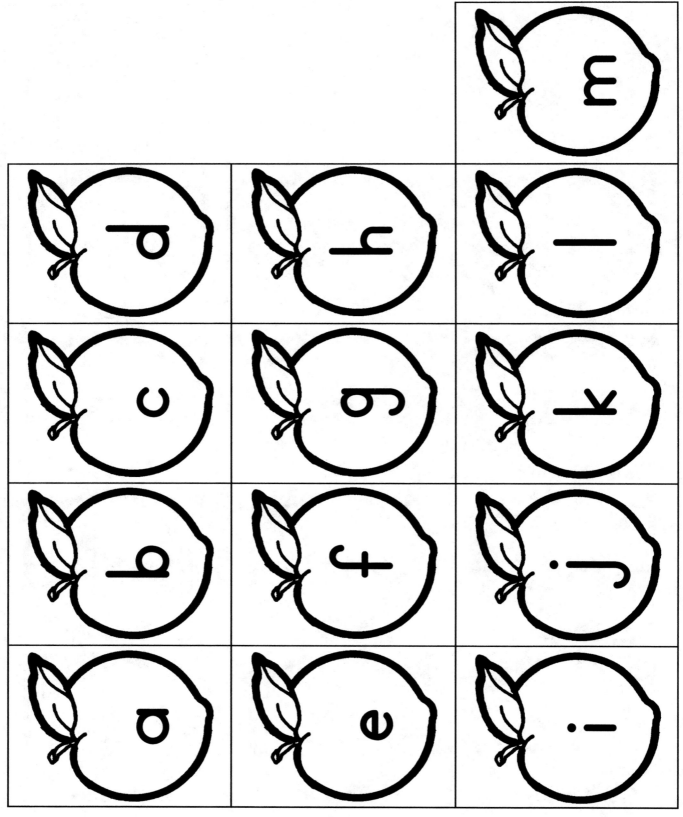

Little Jack Horner (cont.)

Lowercase Letters (cont.)

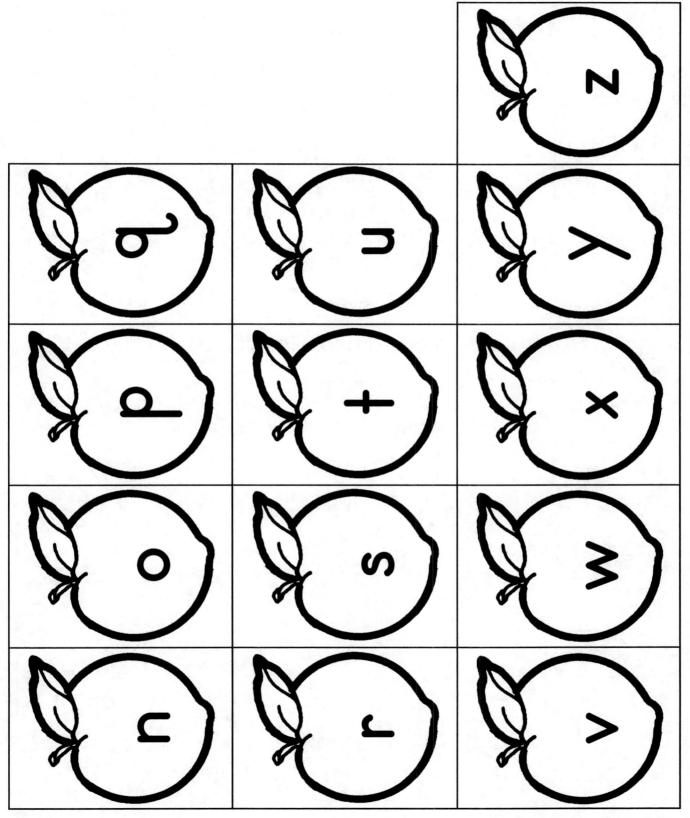

Diddle, Diddle, Dumpling

Diddle, diddle, dumpling,

my son John,

Went to bed with his

trousers on;

One shoe off, the other

shoe on,

Diddle, diddle, dumpling,

my son John.

Diddle, Diddle, Dumpling (cont.)

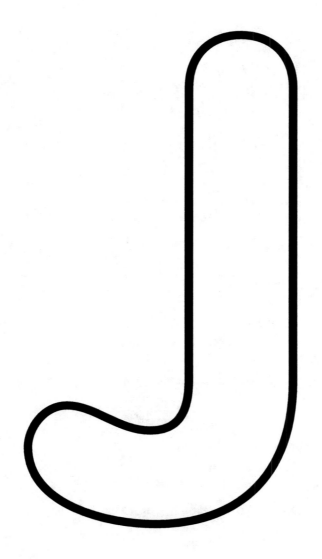

"J," John, Little Dumpling John, had
one shoe off and one shoe on.

Diddle, Diddle, Dumpling *(cont.)*

Lesson

Skill

- syllable segmentation

Materials

- small box or bag
- small items from classroom (pencil, ball, eraser, crayon, flower, cup, necklace, frame, clock), one per student
- syllable activity sheet (page 69), one per student
- chart paper

Before the Lesson

1. Copy the nursery rhyme "Diddle, Diddle, Dumpling" onto chart paper or enlarge it so that the class can see the words easily.

2. Gather small, familiar items having different numbers of syllables. Put an item for each child in the bag or box.

Procedure

1. Read the nursery rhyme "Diddle, Diddle, Dumpling" to the class, using the large display version. Read the rhyme again, tracking the words and allowing the students to join in when they are familiar with the rhyme.

2. Together, count the number of words that are in the rhyme. (26)

3. Explain that each word is made up of letters. The letters form *syllables*. Some words, like *play*, have only one syllable. The word *recess* has two syllables, re—cess. Ask students if they can hear the two different syllables that make up the word "recess." Next, have them clap, stomp, or snap the syllables in their first and last names. Ask them to pair up and share the number of syllables (word parts) in their first names and then their last names.

4. Once the students grasp the concept of syllables, go through the rhyme very slowly. Say the words carefully, so that the students can clap as they repeat each syllable.

5. Repeat the rhyme a second and third time. Try signaling the syllables in different ways (snapping fingers, stomping feet, etc.).

6. One final time, read the rhyme but this time, have the students tell how many syllables (word parts) there are in each word.

7. Next, allow each child to take an item from the bag. Have him or her say, clap, and count the word parts in the item chosen.

8. Assess comprehension of the skill by using the syllable activity sheet.

Diddle, Diddle, Dumpling (cont.)

Directions: Count the number of syllables (word parts) in each picture. Write your answer on the line in each box.

butterfly

shoe

trousers

telephone

acorn

bed

rabbit

cowboy boot

house

Georgie Porgie

Georgie Porgie

Pudding and pie,

Kissed the girls

And made them cry.

When the boys

Came out to play,

Georgie Porgie

Ran away.

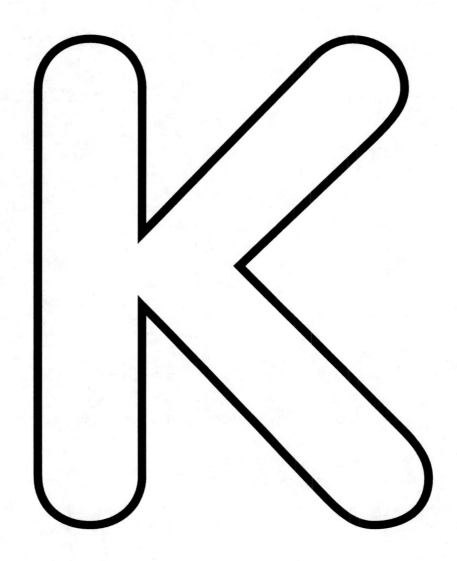

"K," kiss, Georgie Porgie, pudding and pie, kissed the girls and made them cry.

Georgie Porgie *(cont.)*

Lesson

Skills

- letter recognition
- sound recognition

Materials

- instant pudding, one box per 6 students
- wet wipes
- milk
- pie tins, one per student
- butcher paper or chart paper

Before the Lesson

1. Copy the rhyme "Georgie Porgie" onto butcher paper or chart paper so that students can easily view it during the lesson.
2. Have instant pudding prepared and chilled.
3. Have the students wash their hands.

Procedure

1. Read the rhyme "Georgie Porgie" to the class. Track the words as you read them. Reread the rhyme a second time, allowing the students to join in when they are familiar with the words.
2. Pass out wet wipes to each student to allow them to wash their hands. Explain that they will be doing a project with food and that they will get to taste or eat the pudding when they finish with the activity.
3. Ask the students what types of food they heard in the rhyme "Georgie Porgie." (*pudding and pie*)
4. Give each student a pie tin with ³/₄ cup (180 mL) of pudding inside.

5. Say the word "pie." Have the students write the beginning letter "p" in their pudding with their fingers. Continue saying different words until all the letters of the alphabet have been represented and spelled out in the pudding.
6. Allow students to lick their fingers and the pans if they wish.
7. Hand out wet wipes for cleanup and collect the pie plates.

Mary Had a Little Lamb

Mary had a little lamb,

Its fleece was white as snow;

And everywhere that Mary went

The lamb was sure to go.

It followed her to school one day,

which was against the rule.

It made the children laugh and play,

To see a lamb at school.

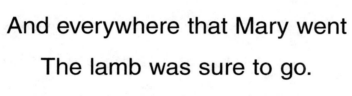

Mary Had a Little Lamb (cont.)

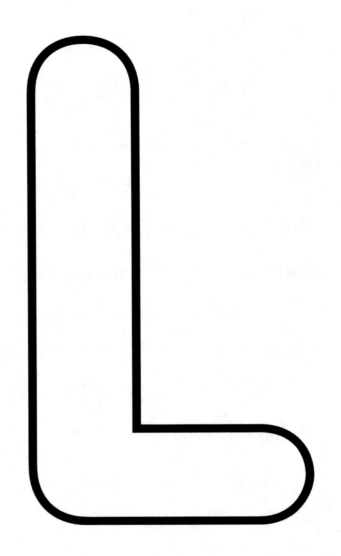

"L," lamb, Mary's little lamb followed her to school. Now she's in a jam.

Mary Had a Little Lamb *(cont.)*

Lesson 1

Skills

- role-playing
- sequencing

Materials

- Finger Puppets (page 76), one per student
- crayons
- scissors
- glue

Before the Lesson

1. Copy the nursery rhyme "Mary Had a Little Lamb" onto chart paper or enlarge it so the class can see the words easily.
2. Copy one puppet pattern page for each student.
3. Arrange materials to prepare finger puppets.

Procedure

1. Read the nursery rhyme "Mary Had a Little Lamb," using the enlarged version of the rhyme. Read the rhyme a second time, tracking the words and allowing the students to join in if they already know the rhyme.
2. Give each student the Finger Puppets page. Instruct the students to color the puppets.
3. Next, cut out the four puppets and fold each one on the dotted line.
4. Place glue along the outside edge of the puppet. Do not place glue along the bottom by the feet. Fold the puppet together and press gently along the glued edges. Smooth the sides and let the puppet dry.

5. Act out the rhyme, using the puppets. Take turns being the different characters in the rhyme.

Extension: Create a puppet theater for students to use.

Mary Had a Little Lamb (cont.)

Finger Puppets

Mary Had a Little Lamb (cont.)

Lesson 2

Skills

- sequencing
- comprehension

Materials

- "Mary Had a Little Lamb" Sequencing Cards, page 78, one per student
- Flip-book Pattern (page 79), one per student
- 8½" x 11" (22 cm x 28 cm) copy paper
- crayons
- glue sticks
- scissors

Before the Lesson

1. Make one copy of the flip-book pattern found on page 79 for each student.
2. Copy the "Mary Had a Little Lamb" sequencing cards for each student.

Procedure

1. Read the nursery rhyme "Mary Had a Little Lamb," using the enlarged version of the rhyme. Read the rhyme a second time, tracking the words and allowing the students to join in.
2. Discuss what *sequencing* means. Explain that when you sequence something, you put it in order. (*first, next, last*)
3. Tell the students that they will be sequencing the rhyme of "Mary Had a Little Lamb," using the cards on their worksheets. They will be deciding what happened first, what happened next, and what happened last. When the cards are arranged in order, they will glue them onto the strip.
4. Then, introduce the flip-book pattern. Show the students how to fold the paper and cut on the dotted lines.
5. When the flip-book page has been folded and cut, have the students glue in the story strip under the numbered flaps.
6. Demonstrate how to lift the numbered flaps and read the story.

Mary Had a Little Lamb *(cont.)*

Sequencing Cards

Directions: Cut out the three picture cards and the number strip. Put the cards in the order they occur in the rhyme. Glue them on the strip and place the completed strip inside the folded flip book.

It followed her to school one day.

It made the children laugh and play.

Mary had a little lamb. Its fleece was white as snow.

3.

2.

1.

Mary Had a Little Lamb *(cont.)*

Flip-book Pattern

Directions: Cut out the pattern. Fold the paper along the solid line. The numbers should be on top. Cut the two dashed lines. Place the completed story strip (page 78) inside.

Little Miss Muffet

Little Miss Muffet

Sat on a tuffet

Eating her curds and whey.

Along came a spider

Who sat down beside her

And frightened

Miss Muffet away.

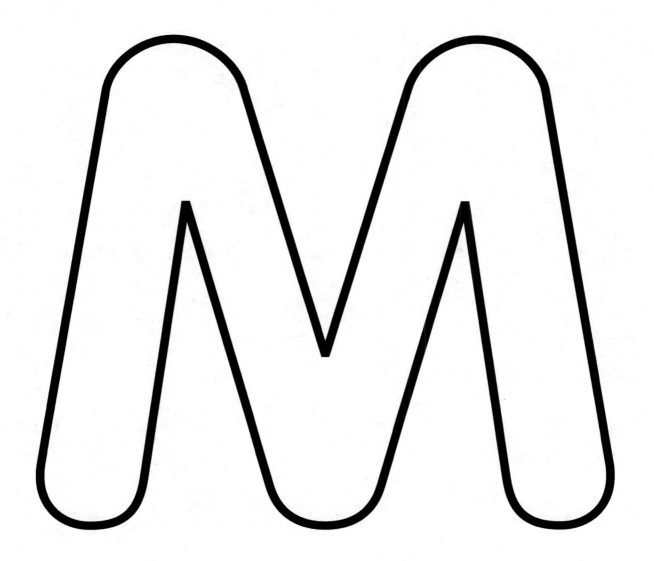

"M," Muffet, Little Miss,
would not give that spider a kiss.

Little Miss Muffet (cont.)

Lesson

Skills

- role playing
- understanding positional words

Materials

- spider puppet pattern (page 84), one per student
- butcher paper or chart paper
- small chair or stool
- construction paper
- scissors
- crayons
- glue

Before the Lesson

1. Copy the rhyme "Little Miss Muffet" onto butcher paper or chart paper so that students can easily view it during the lesson.

2. Copy the spider puppet pattern page for each student. Determine how much cutting the student will be able to do. Cut out necessary parts from construction paper for each student's spider.

3. Create a sample spider to use as a prop for the initial drama.

Procedure

1. Read the rhyme "Little Miss Muffet" to the class. Track the words as you read them. Reread the rhyme a second time, allowing the students to join in.

2. Ask the students to identify words that are new to them in the rhyme. (*tuffet, curds,* and *whey*) Discuss what a tuffet might be. Explain that Miss Muffet sat on a tuffet, which gives us a clue as to its use. (*stool, chair*) Mention that she is eating curds and whey. Suggest to the students that eating curds and whey would be like eating cottage cheese with some milk poured over it.

3. Choose a student who would like to role-play the nursery rhyme for the class. Use a student chair for the tuffet. Allow the student chosen to act out the nursery rhyme in front of the class. Substitute the student's name for Miss Muffet in the rhyme. Example: Little Miss Susie sat on a tuffet, eating her curds and whey…

Little Miss Muffet (cont.)

Lesson (cont.)

Procedure (cont.)

4. Choose another student to act out the nursery rhyme in the same way, but change the positional word "on" to "beside." Example: Little Mr. Jose sat beside a tuffet, eating his curds and whey. Along came a spider and sat down beside him and frightened Mr. Jose away.

5. Continue this activity with the rest of the class by substituting different positional words for "on" (i.e., *around, under, over, between, above* and *below*).

6. Give each child a copy of the spider puppet (page 84). Model for the students how to create the spider puppet.

   • Cut out the correct number of spider parts. Make sure there are eight legs, two head/bodies, two eyes, and one mouth.

   • Glue the eyes and mouth to the front of the spider.

   • Attach four legs to the front of the spider and four legs to the back of the spider.

   • Align the front and back of the spider so that the legs are dangling together. Staple the front to the back along the curve. Leave the flat edge open.

7. After each student has completed his or her puppet, have him or her return to the gathering area. Practice using the puppet by sliding a hand into the "mitt." Repeat the nursery rhyme, using the puppet.

8. Use the puppets to review positional words. *(under, around, between, beside, on, above, and below)*

Little Miss Muffet *(cont.)*

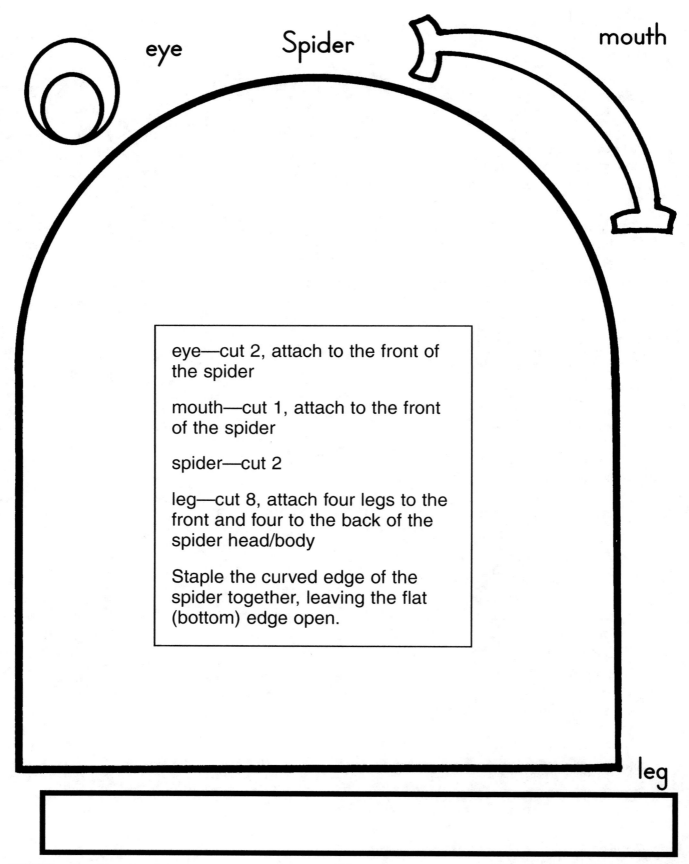

eye   Spider   mouth

eye—cut 2, attach to the front of the spider

mouth—cut 1, attach to the front of the spider

spider—cut 2

leg—cut 8, attach four legs to the front and four to the back of the spider head/body

Staple the curved edge of the spider together, leaving the flat (bottom) edge open.

leg

84   ©Teacher Created Resources, Inc.

Little Nut Tree

I had a little nut tree;
Nothing would it bear
But a silver nutmeg
And a golden pear.

The king of Spain's daughter
Came to visit me,
And all for the sake
Of my little nut tree.

I skipped over water,
I danced over sea,
And all the birds in the air
Couldn't catch me.

Little Nut Tree (cont.)

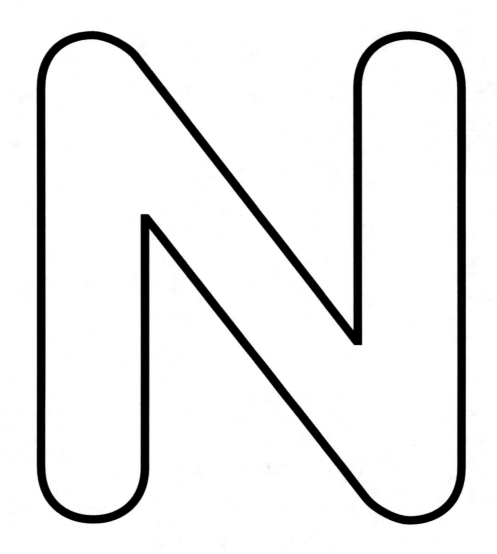

"N," nutmeg, nutmeg and pear,
would my little nut tree bear.

Little Nut Tree *(cont.)*

Lesson

Skill

- letter recognition

Materials

- heavy paper
- peanut butter play dough
- plastic forks, one per student
- small paper cups, one per student
- My Little Letter Tree play dough board pattern (page 88), one per student

Before the Lesson

1. Copy the rhyme "Little Nut Tree" from page 85 onto butcher paper or chart paper and display it so that it can be easily viewed by students during the lesson.

2. Make one My Little Letter Tree play dough board per student. Copy the pattern onto heavy paper and laminate each card.

3. Have the ingredients for peanut butter play dough ready for each student. Use the recipe below.

4. Have students wash their hands.

Procedure

1. Read the rhyme "Little Nut Tree" to the class. Track the words as you read them. Reread the rhyme a second time, allowing the students to join in.

2. Explain to the students that peanuts are also called groundnuts because they ripen underground. Tell them that peanut butter is made with peanuts and that it is possible to make play dough using peanut butter.

3. Give each student a cup of ingredients to make his or her play dough. Have them return to their seats and mix up the ingredients, using a plastic fork.

4. When their play dough is ready, pass out the letter tree boards. Encourage the students to form different letters on the board, using the dough they made. More advanced students can try spelling words.

5. When they have had enough time to create their letters, allow the students to eat their play dough!

Edible Peanut Butter Play Dough

1 tablespoon of peanut butter

2 tablespoons of powdered milk

1 tablespoon of honey

Directions

Stir the ingredients until the consistency is doughlike. Add powdered milk if it is too sticky.

Allergy Alert: Make certain no students are allergic to peanuts before using this recipe.

Little Nut Tree (cont.)

My Little Letter Tree

Old Woman in a Shoe

There was an old woman,

Who lived in a shoe.

She had so many children,

She didn't know what to do.

She gave them all broth

Without any bread;

Then kissed them all soundly

And put them to bed.

Old Woman in a Shoe (cont.)

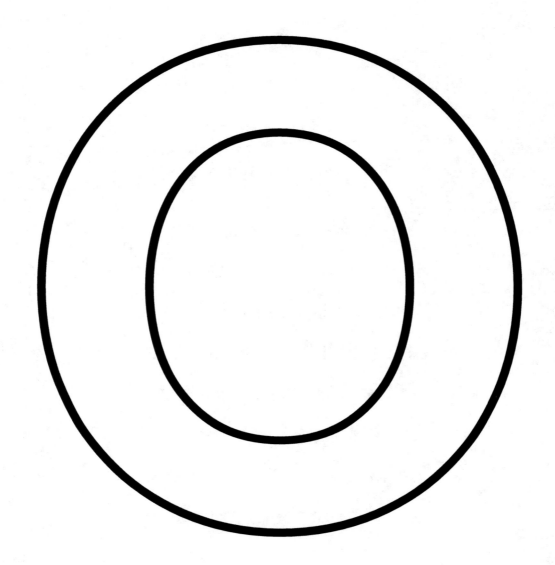

"O," old, old woman in a shoe,
had so many kids, what's she going
to do?

Old Woman in a Shoe (cont.)

Lesson

Skills

- fact/fiction discrimination
- character/setting recognition

Materials

- 3" x 6" (8 cm x 15 cm) sticky notes or index cards
- Character Patterns (page 94), one page per student
- Shoe Pattern (page 93), two per student
- 1 large plastic cup for each student
- shoelace or yarn for each student
- markers or crayons
- chart paper
- hole punch
- scissors
- tape

Before the Lesson

1. Cut out two shoe patterns for each student. Punch holes in the shoes where indicated.
2. Measure yarn if shoelaces are unavailable.

Procedure

1. Read the nursery rhyme "Old Woman in a Shoe" to the class, using the larger display version. Read the rhyme again, tracking the words and allowing the class to join in if they are familiar with it.

2. Discuss this rhyme by asking, "Is this a story that could really happen?" When we read a story that is make-believe, we call it *fiction*. Let's think of some other places for the little old lady to live that are fictional (make-believe) places. (*banana peel, flowerpot, old tire*)

3. Using chart paper and a marker, write the following sentence:

   There was an old lady who lived in a _____.

4. As a student comes up with an answer, write it on a sticky note (or on an index card with tape attached to it.) Allow the student to place his or her idea on the chart under the sentence. Read the new sentence aloud with the class.

   There was an old woman who lived in *a coffee cup.*

5. After several students have had a turn coming up with fictional (make-believe) places that the old woman could live, ask the students to think of places where the old woman and her children might really live.

Old Woman in a Shoe *(cont.)*

Lesson *(cont.)*

6. Using the same chart paper, remove the sticky notes, and begin writing down new student answers which depict places in which the old woman could actually live. Try to allow all students a chance to participate.

   There was an old lady who lived in *an apartment*.

7. After taking several answers, explain that students are going to act out the nursery rhyme. What are the things that will be needed? (*shoe*) What characters do we need? (*children and an old woman*)

8. Show the students the two shoe patterns and the patterns for the children and the old lady. Make certain that the two shoes will match when put together. It may help to mark the side of each shoe pattern that will be colored. Have students color and cut out one of the shoes.

9. Tape a plastic cup to the back of the colored shoe. This will not only hold the shoe up, but it will serve as a storage area for the old woman and her children.

10. Color and cut out the second shoe pattern and tape it to the other side of the cup. Remind the students that a shoe usually looks the same on both sides. The cup should now be hidden between the two colored shoe patterns.

11. Lace the shoes, using the shoelace or piece of yarn. (Adult assistance may be necessary.)

12. When the shoe is complete, begin working on the characters in the rhyme. Ask students what they think is missing in the patterns they have been given. (*faces*) Have the students create faces for the old woman and the children. Color them and cut them out.

13. Recite the nursery rhyme as you use the manipulatives that you have created to reenact this rhyme.

Old Woman in a Shoe (cont.)

Shoe Pattern

Directions: Cut two shoes. Color each shoe, making sure the outsides will be colored when the two are put together.

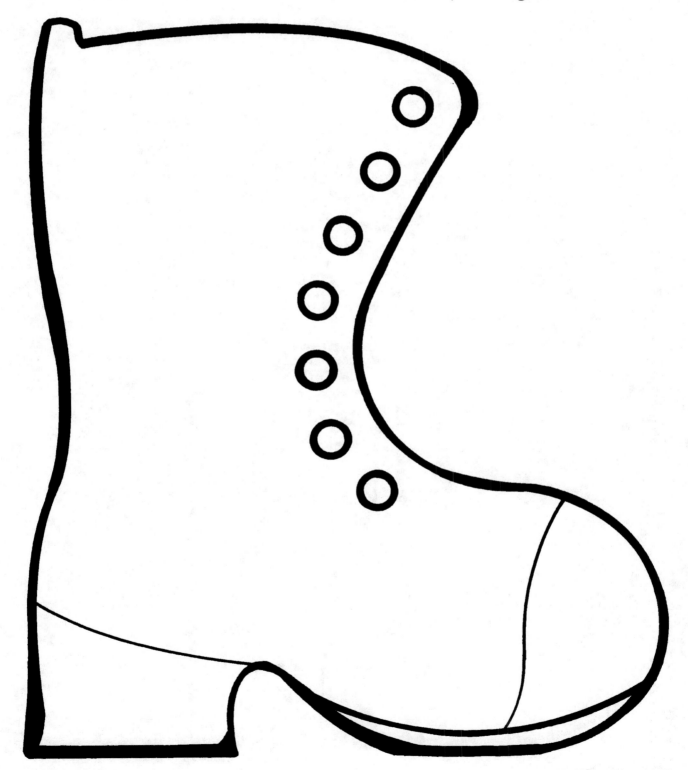

Old Woman in a Shoe (cont.)

Characters

Directions: Draw faces on the characters. Color and cut out the characters for use with "Old Woman in a Shoe" on page 89.

Little Bo-Peep

Little Bo-Peep

Has lost her sheep,

And doesn't know where

To find them.

Leave them alone,

And they'll come home

Wagging their tails

Behind them.

Little Bo-Peep *(cont.)*

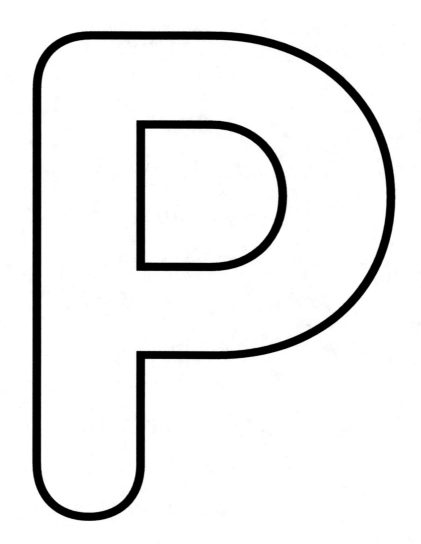

"P," peep, Little Bo-Peep.
If she's not careful, she'll lose
her sheep.

Little Bo-Peep (cont.)

Lesson

Skills

- onsets and rimes

Materials

- animal pictures (page 98)
- chart paper or butcher paper

Before the Lesson

1. Copy or enlarge the nursery rhyme "Little Bo-Peep" onto chart paper or butcher paper so that the entire class will be able to view the rhyme as it is read.

2. Copy, cut apart, and laminate the animal cards. Make half as many cards as students. Then, cut each animal card so that the first sound (*onset*) is separated from the rest of the word (*rime*). (*d*=onset; *uck*=rime)

Procedure

1. Read the nursery rhyme "Little Bo-Peep" to the class. Read the rhyme again, tracking the words on the chart paper, and invite the students who know the rhyme to join in reading it with you.

2. Ask the students where they could go to see sheep. (*farm or farm area at a zoo*)

3. Ask the students to name other animals found on a farm. Write their answers on chart paper.

4. Next, give each student half of an animal picture card. Explain that each student has a card with half an animal and part of a word on it. The object of the game is to find the person who has the other half of the animal and the rest of the word.

5. When all the animal pictures have been matched, have each student share his or her word (*animal*) by saying the rhyme "Little Bo-Peep" but changing the word *sheep* to his or her animal.

Example:

Little Bo-Peep lost her *cow*

and can't tell where to find it.

Leave it alone

and it will come home,

wagging its tail behind it.

Little Bo-Peep *(cont.)*

Directions: Color and cut out the animal cards. Make a jagged cut on each card, dividing them in half, leaving the first sound (onset) on one half and the rest of the word (rime) on the other.

c o w

p i g

c a t

r o o s t e r

h o r s e

d u c k

g o a t

s h e e p

Jack Be Nimble

Jack be nimble,

Jack be quick,

Jack jump over

The candlestick.

"Q," quick, Jack be quick.
Jack jump over the candlestick.

Jack Be Nimble (cont.)

Lesson

Skill

- action word recognition

Materials

- Action Words cards (page 102), one set per class
- a large candle in a candlestick

Before the Lesson

1. Copy or enlarge the nursery rhyme "Jack Be Nimble" onto chart paper or butcher paper so that the entire class will be able to view the rhyme as it is read.

2. Copy, laminate, and cut apart the Action Words cards.

Procedure

1. Read the nursery rhyme "Jack Be Nimble" to the class. Read the rhyme again, tracking the words that have been recreated on chart paper and invite the students who know the rhyme to join in reading it with you.

2. Ask the students what it was that Jack did with the candlestick. (*jumped over it*)

3. Introduce the concept of *action words*. Share that *jumped* is an action word. Brainstorm different action words as a class that Jack could have done over the candlestick. (*hopped, skipped, leaped*) Share the Action Words cards.

4. Introduce the candlestick. Explain that each student will get a turn to go over the candlestick, while the rest of the class says the rhyme. Each student will get a turn to draw a card telling him or her how to go over the candlestick.

5. Begin the game, allowing each student an opportunity to complete an action while going over the large candle and candlestick. Each time a student begins, read his or her card and add the word to the rhyme. Don't forget to change the name in the rhyme, too!

Example:

Katie be nimble,

Katie be quick,

Katie *skipped* over the candlestick.

Variation: Allow the students to pick their own action words when it is their turn while the rest of the class repeats the rhyme.

Action Words

jump	hop	dance
run	leap	skip

Jack and Jill

Jack and Jill

Went up the hill,

To fetch a pail of water.

Jack fell down,

And broke his crown,

And Jill came tumbling after.

Jack and Jill (cont.)

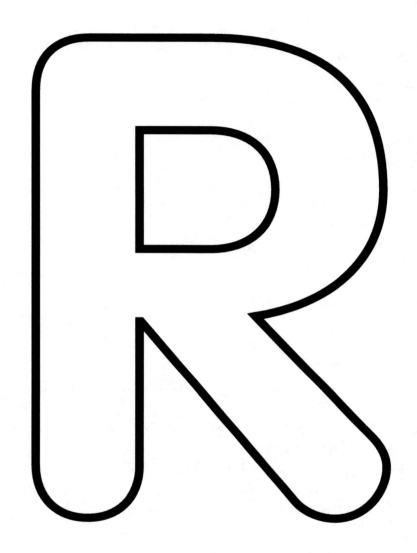

"R," run, run up the hill.

But don't fall down with
Jack and Jill.

Jack and Jill (cont.)

Lesson

Skills
- labeling
- role-playing

Materials
- Jack and Jill labeling sheet (page 106), one per student
- pencil, one per student
- sticky notes

Before the Lesson
1. Copy the labeling sheet onto a transparency.
2. Copy a labeling sheet for each student.

Procedure
1. Read the nursery rhyme "Jack and Jill," using the enlarged version of the rhyme. Read the rhyme a second time, tracking the words and allowing the students to join in if they already know the words.

2. Choose three students to role-play the rhyme. One student will be Jack, one student will be Jill, and the other student will be the pail.

3. Write the words *Jack, Jill,* and *pail* on the sticky notes and have a volunteer place each on the appropriate students. Explain that people and things can have nametags to help us identify them. We call that *labeling.*

4. Have the chosen, labeled students act out the rhyme. When they have finished, they can pass their labels on to other students. Continue until everyone who wishes a turn has had one.

5. Next, tell the students that they are going to help you give the items around the room nametags. One at a time, have each student pick one thing in the classroom to label. With a student's help (possibly beginning and ending letters) write the item's name on a sticky note and allow that student to place it on the chosen item.

6. After every student has had a turn, give them each a copy of the Jack and Jill page and a pencil.

7. As a class, label the picture one item at a time. (*Jack, Jill, pail, hill, sun, grass, flower, cloud*) Write the word next to the item. Connect the word to the picture with a line.

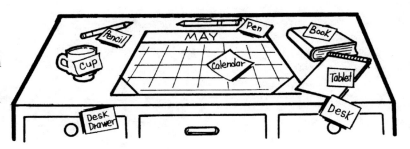

Jack and Jill (cont.)

Word Bank

Jack	hill	flower	pail
Jill	sun	cloud	grass

Simple Simon

Simple Simon met a pieman,

Going to the fair;

Says Simple Simon to the pieman,

Let me taste your ware.

Says the pieman to Simple Simon,

Show me first your penny.

Says Simple Simon to the pieman,

Indeed I have not any.

Simple Simon (cont.)

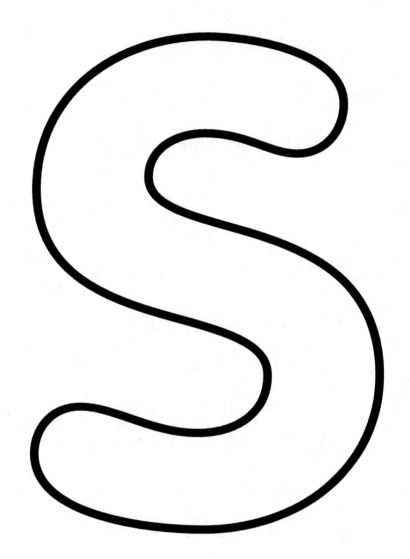

"S," Simon, Simple Simon,
we all know he met a pieman.

Simple Simon (cont.)

Lesson

Skill

- beginning-sound recognition

Materials

- small objects (marble, paperclip, penny, toy car, key, marker, block, etc.)
- pie tins, one for every 3–4 students
- shaving cream
- paper towels

Before the Lesson

1. Copy or enlarge the nursery rhyme "Simple Simon" onto chart paper or butcher paper so that the entire class will be able to view the rhyme as it is read.

2. Put 10–15 small objects in a pie tin for each group of students. Cover the objects with shaving cream just before the class meeting.

Procedure

1. Read the nursery rhyme "Simple Simon" to the class. Read the rhyme again, tracking the words that have been recreated on chart paper and invite the students who know the rhyme to join in reading it with you.

2. Share with the students that Simon met a pieman and wanted to taste a pie. Ask students to share what kind of pies they like. Tell them that you have made a pie and have filled it with all kinds of things.

3. Show the students one of the pies. Share that the pie is not to be eaten but to help learn letter sounds. Put your hand in the shaving cream pie and pull out one object. Name the object and its beginning sound. Put the object on the paper towel and allow a volunteer to pick out another object and name its beginning sound.

4. Next, allow the students to go to their pies and take turns pulling out objects and naming the beginning sounds. Continue in this manner until all the objects have been found in the shaving cream and identified.

5. Have students share their finds with other groups, focusing on the beginning sounds.

Polly Put the Kettle On

Polly put the kettle on,

Polly put the kettle on,

Polly put the kettle on,

   We'll all have tea.

Sukey take it off again,

Sukey take it off again,

Sukey take it off again,

   They've all gone away.

Polly Put the Kettle On (cont.)

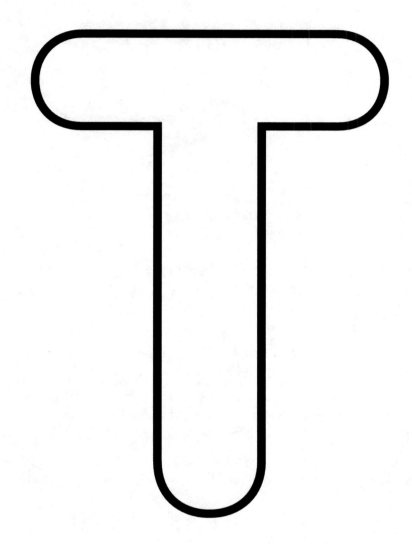

"T," tea, let's all have tea.

Polly put the kettle on for
you and me.

Polly Put the Kettle On (cont.)

Lesson

Skills

- ABC matching
- ordering

Materials

- alphabet activity (pages 114–115)
- teacup and tea bag patterns (page 113)
- string or yarn
- hole punch

Before the Lesson

1. Make 26 copies of the Teacup and Tea Bag pattern page.
2. Make copies of pages 114–115 for each student.
3. Write one uppercase letter (A–Z) on each teacup and one lowercase letter (a-z) on each tea bag.
4. Punch a hole in each cup and attach string or yarn to the cup.

Procedure

1. Read the nursery rhyme "Polly Put the Kettle On," using the enlarged version of the rhyme. Read the rhyme a second time, tracking the words and allowing the students to join in.
2. Give each child a teacup with an upper case letter on it. Some students may need to have more than one cup depending on the class size. If this is the case, try to give the students consecutive letters of the alphabet. (This will make Step 6 a bit less confusing.)
3. Explain that, each student is missing his or her matching lowercase letter. Hold up a tea bag with a lowercase letter on it. The student who has the matching letter on a cup will come up and tape his or her tea bag to the cup.
4. The other students repeat the rhyme "Polly Put the Kettle On" by substituting the student's name for Polly and the letter for the word tea. See example below.

   > Andy put the kettle on.
   > Andy put the kettle on.
   > Andy put the kettle on.
   > Let's all have "J."

5. Repeat this until all the letters have been used.
6. Next, have the students arrange themselves in a line in alphabetical order with their teacup and tea bags.
7. As a follow-up activity, use the teacup worksheets found on pages 114–115 and have the students fill in the missing letters.

Polly Put the Kettle On (cont.)

Teacups and Tea Bags

Directions: Make 26 copies of this page. Add uppercase letters to the teacups. Add lowercase letters to the tea bags.

Polly Put the Kettle On (cont.)

Directions: Fill in the missing uppercase letters on the teacups.

Polly Put the Kettle On *(cont.)*

Directions: Fill in the missing lowercase letters on the tea cups.

Little Boy Blue

Little Boy Blue,

Come blow your horn.

The sheep's in the meadow,

The cow's in the corn.

But where is the boy

Who looks after the sheep?

He's under the haystack,

Fast asleep.

Will you wake him?

No, not I,

For if I do,

He's sure to cry.

Little Boy Blue (cont.)

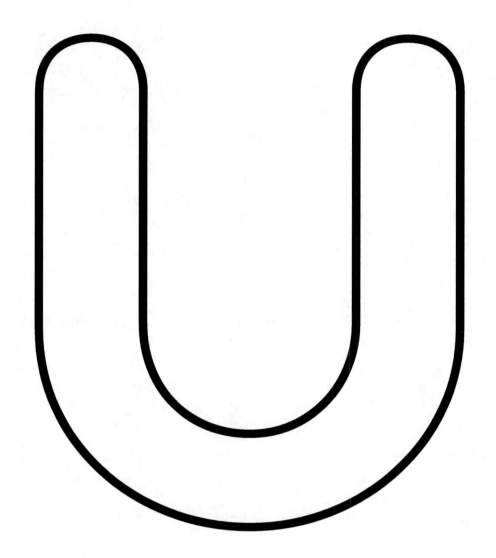

"U," under, under the hay.

Little Boy Blue was sleeping away.

Little Boy Blue *(cont.)*

Lesson

Skill

- understanding cause and effect

Materials

- Cause and Effect activity (page 119), one per student
- scissors
- crayons
- glue
- chart paper

Before the Lesson

1. Make a copy of the Cause and Effect activity for each student.
2. Copy the nursery rhyme "Little Boy Blue" from page 116 onto chart paper or enlarge it so the class can see the words easily.

Procedure

1. Read the nursery rhyme "Little Boy Blue," using the enlarged version of the rhyme. Read the rhyme a second time, tracking the words and allowing the students to join in.
2. Discuss *cause and effect* with the students. Share that Little Boy Blue fell asleep. What happened when he fell asleep? (*Cows got in the corn; sheep are in the meadow.*) Give examples of cause and effect in everyday life.
   - If you brush your teeth (*cause*), you will have clean teeth (*effect*).
   - If you wash your hands (*cause*), you won't spread germs (*effect*).
   - If you don't water the flowers (*cause*), the flowers will die (*effect*).
3. Give the students the Cause and Effect activity page. Have them cut out the effect and glue it to the appropriate cause.

cause

effect

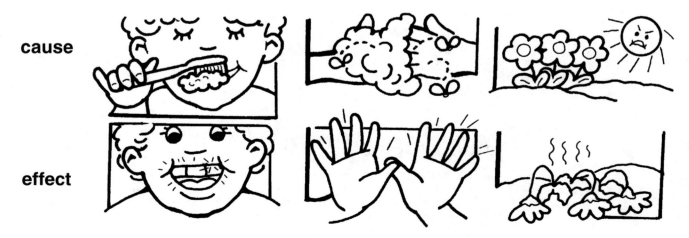

Little Boy Blue (cont.)

Cause and Effect

There Was a Crooked Man

There was a crooked man,

And he walked a crooked mile.

He found a crooked sixpence

Against a crooked stile.

He bought a crooked cat,

Which caught a crooked mouse,

And they all lived together

In a crooked little house.

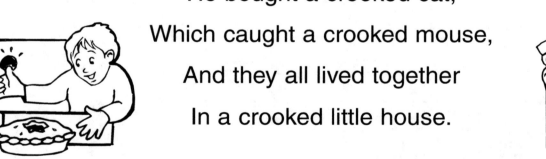

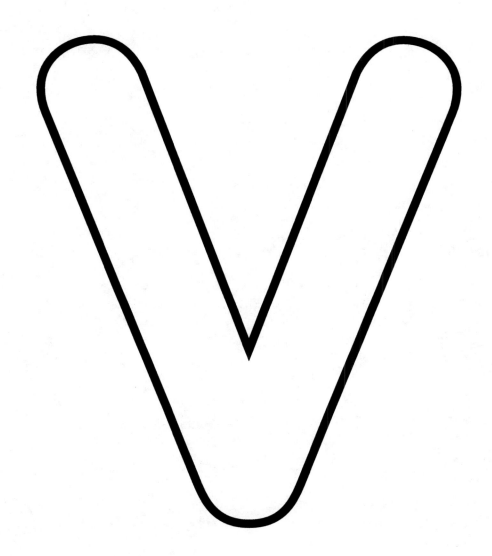

"V," very crooked mouse and a crooked man in a crooked house.

There Was a Crooked Man (cont.)

Lesson

Skill

- reality vs. fantasy (make-believe)

Materials

- real or make-believe activity (page 123), one per student
- butcher paper

Before the Lesson

1. Copy the rhyme "There Was a Crooked Man" onto butcher paper.

Procedure

1. Read the nursery rhyme "There Was a Crooked Man" to the class. Track the words as you read them. Reread the rhyme a second time, allowing the students to join in.

2. Ask the students if the crooked man is *make-believe* or if it could be *real*. Explain to the students that these things could not happen. Things that could not happen are called make-believe. Give make-believe examples from other nursery rhymes.

   - Can a cow jump over a moon?
   - Can a dish and a spoon run away together?
   - Do cats wear mittens?
   - Can children live in a shoe?
   - Do piggies shop at a market?

3. Give students nursery rhyme examples of things that could be *real*. Explain to the students that things that could happen are called real.

   - Could Jack and Jill have gone up a hill?
   - Could Little Boy Blue sleep under a haystack?
   - Could Yankee Doodle ride a pony?

4. Give each student a real or make-believe activity page. Have the students write an "R" next to the picture if it could be real. Have them write an "M" if it's make-believe.

There Was a Crooked Man (cont.)

Directions: Write "R" if it could be real. Write "M" if it is make-believe.

cow over the moon _____

cow eating grass _____

man walking _____

crooked man _____

children in a shoe _____

children in a house _____

piggie shopping _____

piggie in a puddle _____

Humpty Dumpty

Humpty Dumpty

Sat on a wall.

Humpty Dumpty

Had a great fall.

All the king's horses

And all the king's men,

Couldn't put Humpty

Together again.

Humpty Dumpty *(cont.)*

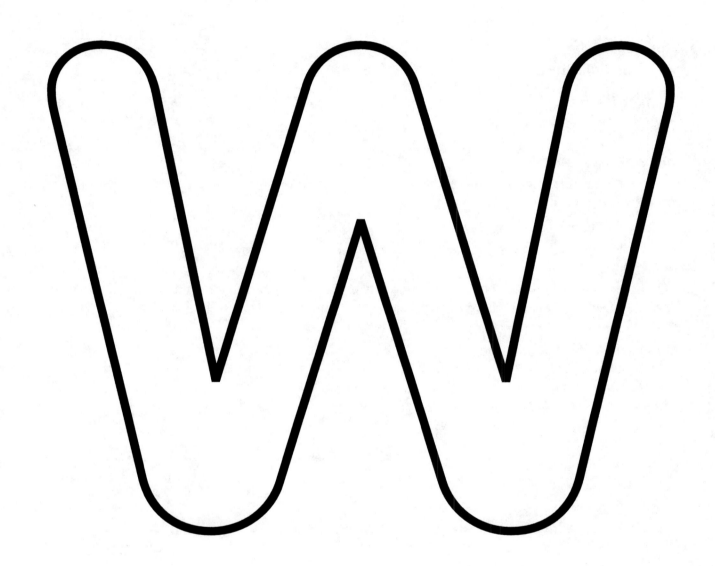

"W," wall, off the wall.

Humpty Dumpty had a great fall.

Humpty Dumpty *(cont.)*

Lesson

Skill

- rhyming words recognition

Materials

- one set of the Rhyming Cards (pages 127–130)
- chart paper
- marker

Before the Lesson

1. Copy the nursery rhyme "Humpty Dumpty" from page 124 onto chart paper or enlarge it so the students can easily see the words.

2. Copy and laminate a set of rhyming cards.

Procedure

1. Read the nursery rhyme "Humpty Dumpty," using the enlarged version of the rhyme. Read the rhyme a second time, tracking the words and allowing the students to join in if they already know the words.

2. Emphasize that Humpty and Dumpty are words that have the same ending sound (but not necessarily the same spelling), therefore they are called *rhyming words*.

3. Read the rhyme again and ask the students to identify other rhyming words.

4. Next, say aloud to the class several pairs of words that rhyme. (*boy-joy; run-fun; bark-shark*) Ask the students to come up with word pairs on their own. Write their suggestions on chart paper for display.

5. Finally, pass out a rhyming card to each student. Each student must find the person holding the card that rhymes with his or her own card.

6. Once everyone has found his or her partner, collect the cards and play again.

Humpty Dumpty *(cont.)*

Rhyming Cards

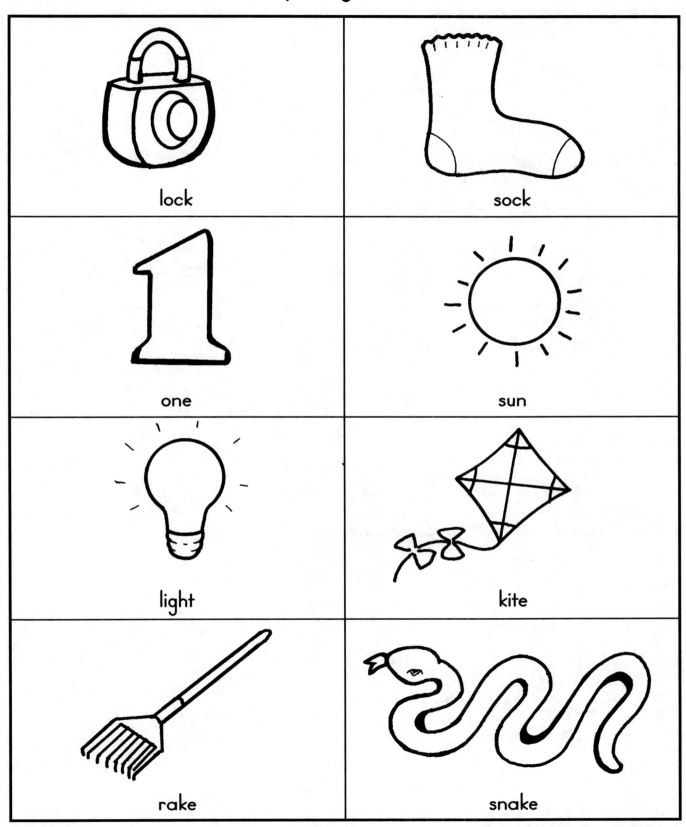

lock	sock
one	sun
light	kite
rake	snake

Humpty Dumpty (cont.)

Rhyming Cards (cont.)

star

car

boat

goat

train

rain

bee

tree

Humpty Dumpty (cont.)
Rhyming Cards (cont.)

hat

bat

spoon

moon

frog

log

mop

stop

Humpty Dumpty (cont.)

Rhyming Cards (cont.)

house

mouse

fish

dish

whale

snail

shoe

two

Baa, Baa, Black Sheep

Baa, baa, black sheep,

Have you any wool?

Yes, sir, yes, sir,

Three bags full.

One for my master,

And one for the dame,

And one for the little boy

Who lives down the lane.

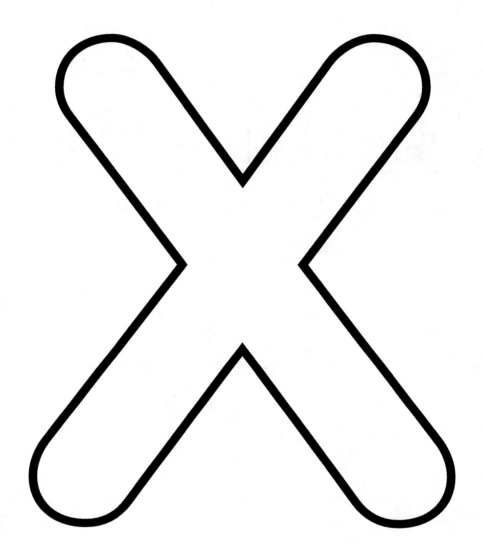

"X," extra, have you any wool?

Yes sir, yes sir, three bags full.

Baa, Baa, Black Sheep (cont.)

Lesson

Skill

- color word recognition

Materials

- coloring activity (page 135), one per student
- Color Word Cards (page 134), one per student
- glue, one small squeeze bottle per student (or group)
- copy paper, one sheet per student
- crayons

Before the Lesson

1. Copy the coloring activity sheet (page 135) for each student.
2. Copy the Color Word Cards (page 134) for each student. Gather glue bottles for each student or group to use.

Procedure

1. Read the nursery rhyme "Baa, Baa, Black Sheep," using the enlarged version of the rhyme. Read the rhyme a second time, tracking the words and allowing the students to join in.

    - Ask the students what color the sheep was in the rhyme. (*black*)
    - Discuss what other colors sheep can be. Share that sheep can be gray, white, or black.

2. Review color words with the students. Look around the classroom to find items of each color mentioned as the Color Word Cards are handed out.

3. Show students how to trace over the letters of a color word leaving a thick line of glue. Have students trace over each word on their Color Word Cards with glue, and let the page dry.

4. When the glue has dried, cut out the cards. Give each student a piece of plain paper to place over the cards. With the appropriate color of crayon, have the students rub on the paper placed over each word card.

5. Have the students color the sheep on page 135. Remind them to use the appropriate color (written below each sheep).

Baa, Baa, Black Sheep (cont.)

Color Word Cards

Directions: Using a small squeeze bottle of glue, trace over the letters of each color word. When the glue dries, cut out the cards. Read each card, find the crayon to match the color word, and make a rubbing of the word. To make a rubbing, lay a piece of paper over each card, and rub over the raised glue area with the appropriate crayon.

black	blue
green	orange
purple	yellow
red	pink

Baa, Baa, Black Sheep (cont.)

Directions: Color each sheep the color shown in the box.

black	blue	brown
green	orange	purple
yellow	red	pink

Yankee Doodle

Yankee Doodle

Went to town

Riding on a pony,

Put a feather in his cap,

And called it macaroni!

Yankee Doodle (cont.)

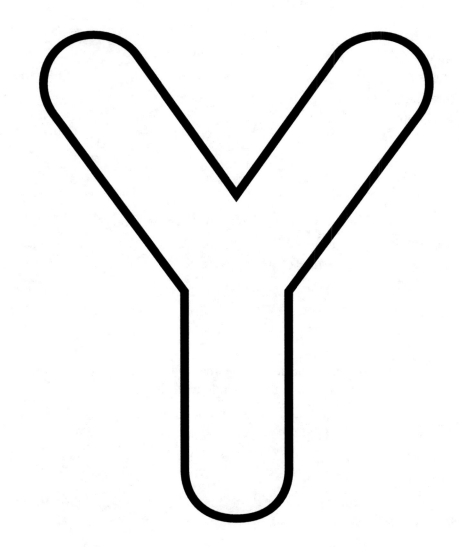

"Y," Yankee, Doodle dee dee,
went to town on his little pony.

Yankee Doodle (cont.)

Lesson

Skill

- sight word recognition

Materials

- Picture Cards (page 139), one set per student
- Word Cards (page 140), one set per student
- butcher paper or chart paper
- envelopes, one per student
- crayons (optional)
- scissors

Before the Lesson

1. Copy the nursery rhyme "Yankee Doodle" from page 136 onto butcher paper or chart paper so that students can easily view it during the lesson.

2. Copy the Word Cards and the Picture Cards for each student.

3. Create a set of Picture Cards and Word Cards to use in the classroom. Color and laminate the cards.

Procedure

1. Read the nursery rhyme "Yankee Doodle" to the class. Track the words as you read them. Reread the rhyme a second time, allowing the students to join in.

2. Pass out the Picture Cards and Word Cards to the students and read the sight words with them. Discuss the pictures and read the picture words.

3. Allow time for students to color and cut out the two sets of cards. Explain that the cards will be used to make sentences.

4. Model a sample sentence using the picture cards and the sight word cards. Have the students create their own sentences and share them with a partner.

5. After the lesson have the students store their pictures and sight words in an envelope to take home. Encourage them to share the activity with their families.

bike

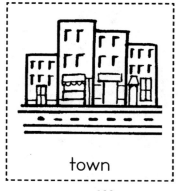

town

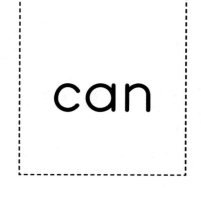

can

Yankee Doodle (cont.)

Picture Cards

Directions: Cut apart the picture cards. Use them with the Word Cards on page 140. Store the cards in an envelope when you are finished making sentences with them.

Yankee Doodle	feather	pony	flag
town	house	flowers	rain
gift	tree	bird	girl
cat	dog	truck	bike

Yankee Doodle (cont.)

Word Cards

Directions: Cut apart the word cards. Use them with the Picture Cards on page 139. Store the cards in an envelope when you are finished making sentences with them.

I	my	it	to
was	is	see	who
what	with	a	can
and	in	on	the

This Little Piggie

This little piggie went to market,

This little piggie stayed at home,

This little piggie had roast beef,

This little piggie had none,

And this little piggie cried,

Wee, wee, wee!

All the way home.

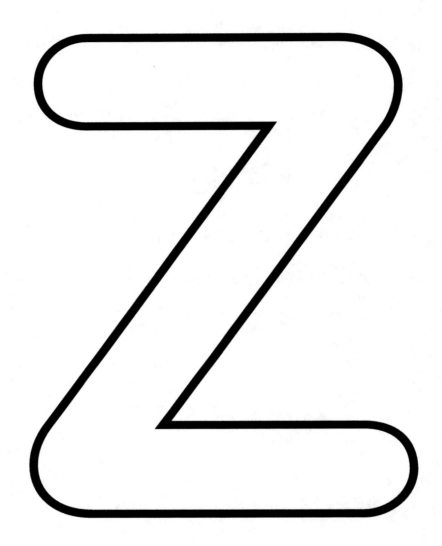

"Z," zero roast beef had he,

for the little piggie who went
wee, wee, wee.

This Little Piggie *(cont.)*

Lesson

Skill

- writing for meaning

Materials

- This Little Piggie's Shopping List (page 144), one per student
- chart paper
- pencils or crayons

Before the Lesson

Copy the nursery rhyme "This Little Piggie" from 142 onto butcher paper so that students can easily view it.

Procedure

1. Read the nursery rhyme "This Little Piggie," using the enlarged version of the rhyme. Read the rhyme a second time, allowing the students to join in if they are familiar with the rhyme.

2. Discuss with the students that the first little piggie went to the market. Explain that a *market* is another name for a grocery store.

3. Ask the students to list some items that their family usually needs from the grocery store. Write the student suggestions on the chart paper.

4. Tell the students that sometimes people forget items that they may need. Ask students to think of a good way to remember all the items needed. *(make a list)*

5. Use chart paper to model a shopping list.

6. Next, pass out one "This Little Piggie's Shopping List" to each student. Have the students create their own grocery lists for the little piggie who went to the market.

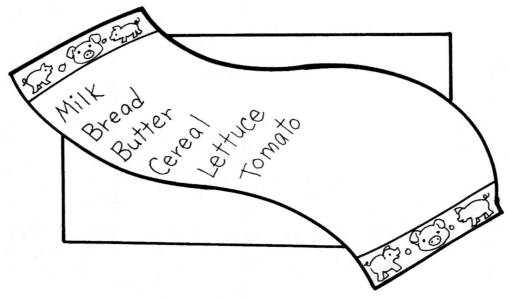

This Little Piggie (cont.)
This Little Piggie's Shopping List